Online Direct Sales
decision framework for manufacturers

by

Wilko Klaassen

November 2010

Submitted in Partial Fulfillment of the Requirements
for the Degree of:

Master of Business Administration (MBA)

Contact information Author:
M2C@wklaassen.nl

First Publication November, 2010

© 2010 by Wilko Klaassen

M2C@wklaassen.nl

ISBN: 978-1-4583-9271-8

Table of Contents

Index of Tables

Index of Figures

Abstract

Manufacturers of branded durable goods that use the internet to sell direct to the consumer may benefit from increased strategic advantage and financial performance, outweighing real (or imagined) "channel conflict" or negative sales cannibalization.

The manufacturer is then able to more effectively balance channel control, strengthen the brand and establish direct consumer relations. An added benefit, as shown by research, of the manufacturer adding direct channel is improved retail service levels, resulting in overall increase of the added value in the channel, with the consumer as the ultimate winner.

The understanding of manufacturer on-line sales engagement and opportunities has not been previously extensively researched. This paper as partial fulfillment of the requirements of the MBA degree, outlines the key issues of on-line direct sales, the role of the single brand store and brings together the latest models.

On-line shopping has transformed the retail business model, as most of the retailers that sell durable goods are also marketing their products on-line, along with the pure internet retailers. The availability and accessibility on product information that Internet provides has increased the consumer power, as they are now in control where and when to buy. The growth of the market has resulted that in 2009 about 30% of the EU-15 consumer bought on-line.

Internet has also sparked the Internet channel conflict, due to the transparency it provides. The channel conflict can be price and/or service driven, and exist within and across the different sales channels, as the different resellers in the same market are competing for the same consumer. Research shows, retailers that have added a channel resulted in increased strategic and financial performance.

The problem that manufacturers of durable goods are facing is how to decide, in a structured approach, on their on-line sales strategy that defines the level of engagement with on-line sales in the different markets, and leverage from their brand value. They see the need of being engaged on-line and understand the complexity that differs, by market and brand. Most manufacturers have taken the first steps by selling direct accessories and spares to the consumer, only that is not their core business and where the real sales and margin opportunities are present. Only a limited group of manufacturers have decided to sell their core products direct.

To understand suitability of their goods for on-line sales the manufacture must analyze the level of web appropriateness of their products, as this will be a key driver behind if the products can be sold on-line. The brand strategy is another key element to take into account, as the brand will be the key driver for traffic or the on-line sales strategy can strengthen the brand, for both a good understanding is needed for what drives the consumer to buy from a single brand store. To get this consumer insight a field survey has been conducted for this paper and the results are presented in chapter 4.

The research, as used for providing a structured solution, shows that the manufacturer can adopt several on-line sales strategies from cooperation to conflict. By deciding on the strategy there is also a need to address the potential conflicts and level of potential damage resulting from the decision to the business that arise from the on-line sales strategy decision and how to mitigate this risk. During the decision phase the manufacturer must also understand the value of, and define the use of the direct consumer data that becomes available when interacting directly with the end user.

A decision framework is provided to assist manufacturers entering the on-line sales market. This framework is presented in Figure 29 on page 83, the aim of this framework is to collect the right information to make the best strategic decision and develop the implementation plan.

1 Introduction

As part of the Euro*MBA exist the requirement to write a final thesis, that covers the different topics studied and how to apply these to a business challenge. The topic of this thesis is mainly a Business Consulting Project that looks into business challenges and opportunities for direct sales, supported by actual cases, literature studies and field surveys.

1.1 Rationale of Study

The development of Internet and the consumers' acceptance to transact on-line, resulted in that the European 2010 estimate is that about 5,5% of all consumer purchases (value) were made via the on-line sales channel. This has been a sales growth in the last 12 months of about 20% compared to 2009. Total retail growth shows a 1,4% sales increase for the same period, according to the CRR in February 2010 (Reuters, 2010)

The development of shopping on-line has been following the development and growth of the Internet. In the early 1990's when the commercial Internet was launched, soon after that event the first commercial transactional websites came available, mainly to place orders on distance. According to an article on Buzzle.com the first web shop to order books was launched in 1992 by C. Stack in the USA, Pizza Hut launched an on-line pizza ordering service in 1994, soon after the now biggest e-commerce sites eBay (first launched as Auctionweb) and Amazon launched in 1995 their first shopping sites in 1995.

Direct sales by a manufacturer took a year longer, Dell launched in 1996 their first direct to consumer transaction website, at the end of the first year they were selling for about 1mln US Dollar a day.

Limited information is available on which was the first consumer brand that started selling direct to the consumer on the web, the pioneers seems to be Apple in 1997, in 2000: Levis, Compaq, Toshiba, Canon and Sony (via Sonystyle.com). One of the reasons why little to no information about manufacturers selling direct is available is due to the sensitivity of selling direct to consumers by a brand owner or manufacture, the earlier mentioned manufacturers sold mainly excess inventory or limited ranges. Most of the manufactures have not taken the step to sell direct, this can be because of several reasons, as they don't see a need, not expecting any business benefits or don't want to cause any channel conflicts between the existing (retail) customers and their own direct channel to consumers.

The problem that manufacturers are facing is how to decide in a structured approach on the level of engagement with on-line sales in the different markets. They see the need of being engaged on-line and understand the complexity that differs by market and brand. They are looking for the best strategy to establish an (direct) on-line sales channel, by avoiding negative effects on their current and future business performance.

The target audience is companies that manufacturer branded goods that want to sell direct,

Some manufacturers have taken the first steps by selling direct accessories and spares to consumers. Most of them are struggling on the why and how of selling their main branded products, mainly due to the risk that direct sales will have a negative effect on their results, due to potential channel conflicts, that will not be compensated by the direct channel.

Within the literature and business books there is to the author's knowledge no guidance or "toolkit" available that addresses all the different steps and possibilities for a go to market model for direct consumer sales.

This leads to the topic of this thesis to analyze what are the potential on-line sales strategies for manufacturers. The aim is to create insight in the possible strategies for manufacturers to sell on-line. Based on that provide a guide for the manufacturers that plan to sell directly to the consumer via their on-line brand stores. This leads to a greater understanding of the benefits and risks of having an on-line sales strategy for the manufacturer and expectations from the consumer.

1.2 Problem statement

The problem statement will throughout this paper have a clear focus and will result in recommendations and framework for the manufacturers that wants to sell direct on-line to consumers. To guide the research and structure the problem statement is support by some research objectives. The problem statement for this study is the following:

Internet provides the manufacturer of branded durable goods direct access to the consumer to promote and sell their products, the problem that the manufacturer faces is how to benefit from this opportunity, with maintaining retailer relations (avoiding channel conflicts), and having a positive effect on the company results for a long term, what are the possible strategies, roadmap and organizational implications and decision criteria to sell direct.

1.3 Research objectives and Questions

The following research objectives and questions will be guidance for and dealt with in the different chapters to reach an answer to the problem statement:

- Evaluate the current state of e-commerce, with specific focus on manufacturers of durable branded goods.
- What do the consumers expect from direct sales by brand owners?
- Analyze reasons for channel conflicts and how can they be avoided?
- What criteria and rational are available for manufacturers to sell direct?
- What are the organizational implications for a manufacturer to work as a retailer?
- How is the manufacturer brand experienced in relation to direct sales by consumers?
- Recommend a framework for manufacturers to guide them on how to develop their on-line direct sales.

1.4 Research framework and Methodology

As preparation for this topic the author conducted pre-research on the urgency and actuality of the topic. The research was based on the author's own knowledge from following the e-commerce market for about ten years out of personal and business interest and collecting relevant articles. This initial research showed that there is little to no relevant research available on manufacturers selling direct to consumers.

The literature that is available on manufacturers' direct sales covers sub-parts that influence the set-up and market approach, like channel conflicts, e-commerce readiness, etc. but these are more generic and retailer focused. The author has followed this development for some time now, and there are some common practices but for sure there is no "tailored" best practice direct sales model available.

The analysis and recommendation will be mainly based on literature research, consumer and professional insight, see Figure 1 for the research framework structure

Research Framework

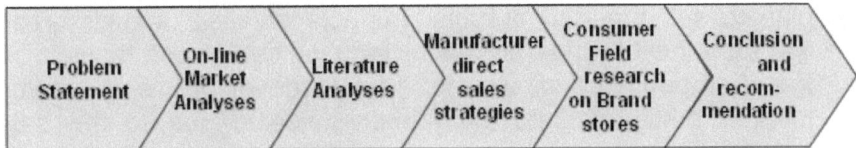

Figure 1 - Thesis research framework

The chapters are structured in line with the above framework.

Chapter 1   Introduction and problem statement

Chapter 2   Literature review and initial analysis

Chapter 3   Focus on the manufacturer and Internet sales strategies

Chapter 4   Consumer field survey analyses

Chapter 5   Framework recommendation for developing the direct sales strategy

The consumer field study results are to be found in chapter 4.

The professional survey, resulted in a limited reach and response mainly due to the fact there are currently only a few professionals who have this experience with selling direct to consumers by a manufacturer, as this has given a limited input the input has been rather consistent and in line with the feedback the author received as direct input form two direct selling manufacturers, this makes the total input based on about eleven professionals that are experienced and qualified to talk about this topic.

The survey questions for both surveys can be found in the Appendix 1 and Appendix 3 starting on page 86.

At the end of the thesis on page 99 the table of consulted books, journals and web pages is available. Reference to the web pages is made throughout the paper by using [xx] where the number refers to the index of consulted web pages.

1.5 Limitations

For clarification there are constraints and limitations of what is covered in this paper, the focus is on manufacturers that sell or plan to sell branded durable products on-line via their brand websites, next to their normal distribution set-up and focus is on the (European) countries that have a developed e-commerce market, these markets have been selected due to the data availability.

The insight gained from the questionnaires provide a good impression on how the consumer thinks about single brand stores, and also the professional view on selling on-line by manufacturers, both have as limitation that they are limited in reach and not representing the average demographics.

2 Literature review

This chapter will cover the literature to develop the market and academic insight needed for developing the recommendation. The literature review will focus on a few areas like:

Market development, as mentioned in the introduction the on-line sales development is closely related to the penetration and usage of Internet, and consumer trust in on-line transactions.

Product fit, not all products can be sold online there needs to be a certain fit to make them attractive enough for consumer to buy them online, this needs to be understood.

What are the different sales channels provided by retail and how do consumers decide what channel they use for research and what channel for purchase? The manufacturer is facing all the different channels, how do they make sure they reach the consumer in a consistent way with their brands.

2.1 e-Commerce in Europe

The European e-commerce market has strongly developed over the past 10 years, the main drivers for this development have been:

- Availability of Internet, the availability of fast Internet (ADSL/Broadband) has given it an additional spur.
- Trust in purchasing online, more secure and better consumer protection.
- Availability of (local) payment methods creating increased trust.
- Improved consumer services and lower cost for delivery as part of the on-line retailers increased professionalism.

The UK, Netherlands, Germany, and Scanidinavian markets have always been leading the development in the European market, two of the main reasons are that these markets were early adaptors of the Internet, and they have a history in distance shopping by using catalogues, so it is not uncommon for the consumer to shop on distance.

The Eurostat (2010) data as presented in Figure 2 shows that the more frequently the Internet is accessed there is also a higher penetration on e-commerce. Exceptions are the Eastern European markets, these are relative young e-commerce markets and have not yet build the consumer trust for buying on-line or having the payment methods available to make it easy.

E-commerce vs. internet usage
Europe by country

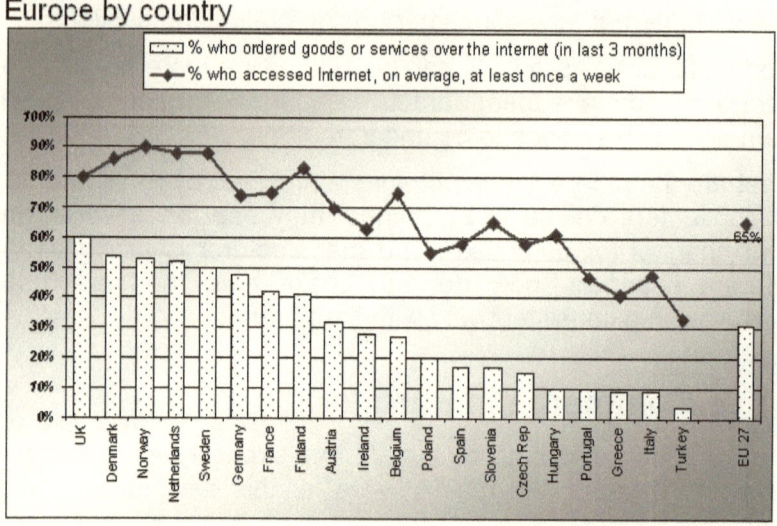

Source: Eurostat Survey on ICT Usage

Figure 2 - E-commerce vs. Internet usage in Europe (Eurostat, 2010)

Convenience is one of the key reasons that e-commerce develops quicker in certain product groups. Other reasons are linked to the product availability and the long tail as described and coined by Chris Anderson (2006). The long tail is making products available on-line that are not profitable to carry for a single local shop, while the online marginal cost for some products is close to zero. One other important element is price, many products are sold for a lower price on the Internet compared to the stores. This can be explained by difference in the cost structure e-tailers can work with a lower margin to cover their cost and still resulting in a good business result.

Anybody that wants to sell on-line needs to understand what is being sold in the market where they want to launch an online shop, in general services and apparel are always the two main categories that consumer orders most on-line. Figure 3 shows the current distribution of products categories for the EU27 average (Eurostat, 2011). The product groups that since 2004 have shown the biggest growth are Household goods (e.g. furniture, toys, etc.) and Software (games etc.), the durable goods are all well presented and are one of the fastest growing products groups bought on-line. Keeping in mind that the durable goods like electronics in general represent a high value, this makes the share of total on-line spend, one of the major categories, together with travels.

Buying different types of products online

% of individuals who ordered the following products or services over the internet in the last 12 months, EU 27 average

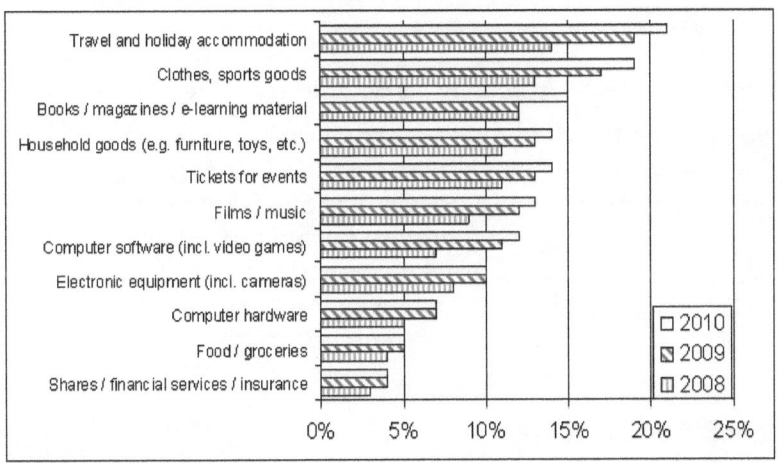

Source: Eurostat Survey on ICT Usage 2010

Figure 3 - Buying different types of products online

The total global e-commerce market has not yet reached its growth limits and more and more consumers will shop on-line, Figure 4 shows a forecast of the expected growth in Europe. The percentage of consumers (EU-15) who shop online is to be expected to reach close to 50% by 2015. Compared to the actual 2009 this is an increased growth of people who order goods online of 44% based on the Eurostat (2010) data.

Online Shopping Forecast

% individuals who ordered goods or services, over the internet, for private use, in the last 3 months, forecast based on actuals 2002/2010

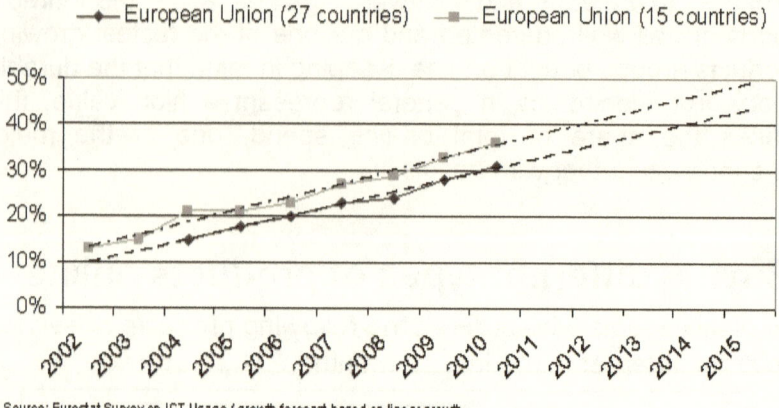

Source: Eurostat Survey on ICT Usage / growth forecast based on linear growth

Figure 4 - E-commerce forecast in the EU (Eurostat, 2010)

To summarize the data as discussed in this paragraph indicates that the e-commerce market has not yet reached its limits. A company not being partly or fully engaged in the e-commerce market and that sell goods that are suitable to sell on-line would result in missing out on a great sales and growth opportunity, the possibility to get in direct contact with the consumer to offer their products and receive direct consumer feedback.

Single European Market

The European Union has set out to develop one single consumer market, this provides the consumer the opportunity to buy in any of the member states. The traditional retail market does not offer that opportunity for the consumer due to the physical distances. In an article by Brook and Pioch (1996), they indicated that the only channel for internationalization would be the distance shopping channel. Interesting enough the distance shopping channel has by now almost totally evolved from catalogue to e-commerce retailers. Some of the biggest retailers that sell pan-European are on-line retailers. This indicates another opportunity for manufacturers to reach all consumers in the EU in a cost efficient and harmonized way, across borders via their own online to consumer platform offering all products and services.

2.2 **Product web appropriateness**

Not all products have a good fit to sell on-line, but the abilities of the e-commerce platforms and the fulfillment solutions have developed tremendously during the last few years, this has expanded the product range that can be offered on-line.

Still a number of products are not that suitable for on-line sales, or for sure will also need physical presence, in the article by Choi et al. (2009) the product appropriateness for the web is discussed. Their approach is that not all products are suitable for web sales. Choi et al. (2009) quotes Figueiredo (2000): "Web appropriateness refers to the extent to which a customer psychologically perceives the products or services as being suitable for web retailing".

For example a product that the consumer feels a strong need to touch or feel will have al low web appropriateness, as the web cannot offer the physical touch and feel it will make the product less suitable for on-line sales. Commodities have for example a high web appropriateness as consumer requires little to none physical interaction with the product. For such products the purchase on-line carries little risk product wise and they can be easily sold on-line.

The touch and feel aspect is not the only aspect that defines the web appropriateness; other elements are:

- The cost of shipment in relation to the product value
- Time to delivery, some products need to be directly fulfilled (fresh food for example), while for others the delivery time is of little importance
- Need for product instructions and information, personal advice
- General availability, time and distance for locating the product (long tail)
- Price sensitivity linked to demand and availability

Additionally not all products can be sold in the same way on the web and will need different organizational approaches, as Choi et al. (2009) puts it: "In addition, it cannot be expected that the firms selling different products or services can all be managed effectively by using the same strategies".

Today's reality is that almost all products are sold or offered on-line with different fulfillment and/or rich media presentation models, this availability results in that more and more consumers purchases or at least researches products they are looking to buy on-line.

The web appropriateness plays an important role in defining the companies' web usage and channel strategy, this to be further explored in the channel conflict management part of this thesis.

2.3 European multi channel development

The distribution channels for manufacturers have developed over time from starting with a single sales channel, quite often the long established manufacturers started with a single direct to consumer channel, into a number of channels operated by different retail companies. Each channel has its own purpose and added value towards delivering products and services to the end user (consumer), see Figure 5 for a traditional channel structure.

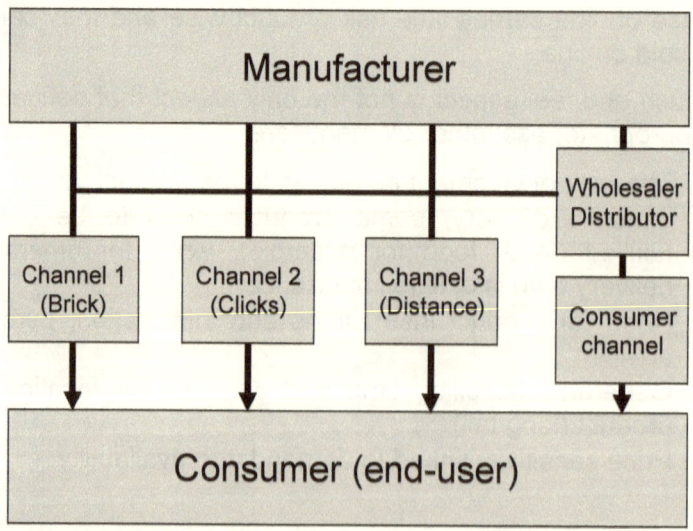

Figure 5 - Channel structure

The manufacturer utilizes the retailer distribution as it would be in most cases to expensive to develop and maintain their own consumer sales and services points. The retailer will utilize the channel or combination of channels that delivers the best results towards their set goals. The manufacturer sales channel strategy aims to find the best match for his sales and marketing strategy.

There is a shift between who holds the power in the sales column, between manufacturer, retailer and consumer. In the beginning the power was with the manufacturer, they had the supply power, ability to deliver goods to the market. Later the power shifted to the retailers, as they had the assortment power, providing the consumer with more choice. With the upcoming of the Internet the power is shifting to the consumers as they have the information power, they can find, compare and decide where to buy by using the information found on the Internet.

This shift in power balance drives companies to transform in how to run their business, as they need to reach and satisfy the consumer. A quote by Umit Kucuk and Krishnamurthy (2007) states: "This fundamental shift threatens the intrinsic informational asymmetry between corporation and consumers and promises to redefine the nature of the company – consumer relationship."

Therefore it is for the manufacturer of paramount importance to understand what channels to use and who holds the power. This should be based on consumer insight, by investigating how consumer behavior changes by using the Internet.

Within and across the channels often conflicts or power struggles occur; channel power has been defined by Stern and El Ansary (1988) as used in the article by Dupuis (1996):

"Power is the ability of one channel member to get another channel member to do what the latter would not otherwise have done. Power is the inverse of dependence: the more highly dependent one channel member is on another, the more power the latter has relative to the other"

The manufacture must strive to optimize the channel management to reach the optimal sales balance and result from the channel mix. Each additional channel that a manufacturer would conclude agreements with has a potential risk of conflicts.

Choi et al. (2009) quote Gaski (1984) on the definition of a channel conflict: "The channel conflict is a situation in which one channel member perceives the other channel member to be engaged in behavior that prevents or impedes him from achieving his goals".

Channel conflicts are common when the manufacturer is distributing his product via different channels or channel players into the same market. The retail partners will not all have the same business model and will compete with each other. The manufacturer will try to manage as good as possible with harmonized pricing and service offering to avoid any conflict, as much as possible.

The channel conflict occurs within or across the channels and can be price or service driven, as the retailers will offer the same product and they can differentiate with the service levels and prices. The manufacturer will manage the retailer behavior by pricing and service options that fit their product marketing and channels best, to make sure the products are marketed in their preferred way in the market and reduce potential channel conflicts.

The other risk manufacturers' face is that when an agreement with a retailer is made, at time of the agreement the retailer was selling through one or more known channels, but afterwards adds another channel like an on-line channel. Many sales agreements do not cover such a change and it is often difficult to take action on. Most retail agreements now concluded include certain conditions, on how the product needs to be marketed and what services need to be present.

A paper by Iyer (1998) highlights another important issue that the nature of the retail competition can be a channel conflict by itself, as the manufacturer and the retailer can have different views on what is causing the conflict; the price or the service. As Iyer (1998) states: "A manufacturer might find the retailers excessively biased either towards price competition at the cost of service provision or vice-versa."

Before on-line sales the channel structure that the manufacturer had to manage was single channel based, see Figure 5, one retailer selling in a consistent way to the consumer. Some retailers operated different channels like a distance sales (catalogue) and retail shops but these were not in conflict with each other. Within in the channel structure a specific channel partner is the wholesaler or distributor. The manufacturer cooperates with them in most cases in markets where the manufacturer is not well established, it is financially not sound to maintain their own distribution network or to supply to smaller retailers that would be to expensive to serve direct.

The latest addition to the channels is the on-line shop. They have been developing not only in sales, but also in professionalism and acceptance for the last 3-5 years.

Nowadays there are several professional shops active in the on-line sales channel. These shops offer almost all multi brands and products; only a few are specialized in a single product category

The on-line shops can be categorized and affiliated with other shops in three groups:

1. Distance sales by using paper catalogue, this category is declining in most markets, and shifting into the on-line sales
2. Multi channel sales by combining an on-line and traditional shop (also known as brick and clicks), this under the same retail brand.
3. On-line sales only, no traditional shop activities (click only or so called pure players)

Internet has not only enabled sales on-line, but it has removed any physical barriers to access product information, like price and where to buy. This access has caused the biggest change for the retailers as business was not just anymore local. Before Internet the channel conflicts were limited to a limited geographic area, as consumers would not travel long distance to make a purchase or they would not even be able to find information about the different prices in the market place.

The upcoming of Internet and on-line sales have changed the retail landscape forever, as the on-line retailer works with a different business model, with different associated cost. When the first on-line shops opened some scholars mentioned that the cost of information, communication and distribution where close to be zero, it is now better understood and also clear that on-line sales is a business model by itself, with different associated cost than traditional retail. The product category sold defines a major part of the on-line shop cost, in most cases the presentation and distribution cost are making the major difference, specially comparing between the tangible and intangible goods and services.

The difference in the cost model and how the products are priced online have as a direct result that the products in most cases are cheaper on-line than in the traditional retail. This causes increased channel conflict and many retailers demanded from manufacturers to take action towards the difference in pricing. The key drivers behind the price differences can be identified by the following two reasons:

1   Lower cost base and this benefit is priced into the consumer pricing, the on-line retailer does not provide in most cases a physical location to experience the products, not having such showrooms and staff results in a lower cost to sales.
2   Difference in pricing approach, not all inclusive, but offering different service levels that are priced along the check-out process, this results that that the initial price looks lower than the final total price at check-out, for example cost for payment, delivery and insurance are added.

The Internet channel conflict is a specific channel conflict as it takes in most cases directly share from the existing traditional channels. Choi et al. (2009) refers to Buckling (1997) in defining the Internet Channel conflict: "The Internet channel conflict occurs when either the Internet or the traditional channel targets customer segments that have been already been served by the other".

The risk of Internet channel conflict has a strong relation with the web appropriateness of the product. Products with high web appropriateness are likely to cause a higher level of conflict compared to products with low web appropriateness. This relation can be easily explained as when the products are not interesting for consumer to buy on-line, there will be little to no offering of these products on-line.

When the first e-commerce activities started most retailers and manufacturers had no idea how to react to this new way of selling, in the article by Burt and Sparks (2003), they quote Katros (2000): "Retailers have worked through the stages of shock, denial, anger, grief and acceptance in coping with the Internet, and are now rushing to identify and secure ways to protect their customer relationship franchise"

For the retailers to get a good understanding on how to work with on-line sales they need to understand the different characteristics that selling on-line have compared to the traditional retail business. In Table 1 are the main characteristics listed that the retailers need to understand and have the skill set for to be successful on-line.

Table 1- Characteristics of new commerce (Dawson, 2001)

Characteristics of the new commerce
(Adapted from Dawson (2001) by Burt and Sparks (2003))
1. New commerce companies operate through multiple marketing channels.
2. Channel structures in new commerce are intermediated in new ways.
3. New commerce retailers operate internationally.
4. New commerce uses new forms of non price competition.
5. In new commerce, organizational scale and scope economies become more important than establishment scale and scope economies.
6. New commerce companies do not subscribe to a traditional view of a difference between goods and services.
7. New commerce companies are using the convergence of information and communications technologies as a primary source of innovation.
8. New managerial ideas support innovation processes.
9. Customer loyalty is a central concept in new commerce.
10. Public sector policies relate to old commerce not new commerce.

E-commerce drives a process of innovation in the retailing, this process innovation pushed for transformation to keep the consumer happy and interested in visiting and purchasing the traditional shops, else the on-line sales will take over an increasingly growing share of the sales from the traditional shops.

A good example of this transformation is the number of travel agents that have closed over the number of years due to the easiness of booking on-line, and most of the travel shops have transformed into specialized travel advisors. The pure selling of flights and hotels are now mainly being sold by the on-line travel agents, like Expedia.com or Hotel.com. A similar trend can now be witnessed in the retail sector, as the on-line sales channel is a clear threat to traditional retail.

As stated by Burt and Sparks (2003): "The threat to established retail and distribution channels, systems and behaviors arises because of the process innovation inherent in e-retailing.".

The retail innovation shows one clear trend, that almost all retailers are going to have a multi channel set-up, existing of a physical location and an on-line shop. These changes have a positive effect on the availability of goods and on the price stability.

Multi channel (see Figure 6) differs from what is most common today that a retailer operates more than one channel independent of each other.

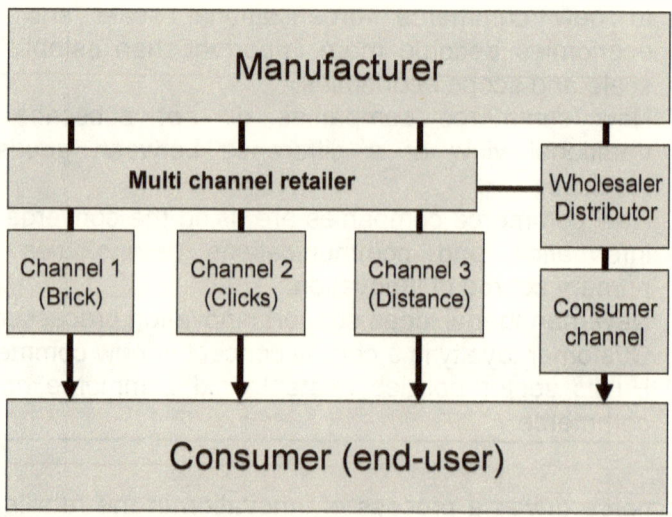

Figure 6 - Multi channel retailer structure

Multi channel retailing is operating multiple channels by a single retailer in an almost seamless connection. The consumer that is shopping with a multi channel retailer will experience a unique but differentiated experience, gathered towards the specific channel that the consumer has accessed. The online magazine retailonlineintegration.com listed in table 2 the most important characteristics of a successful multi channel retailer:

Table 2 - Characteristics of a successful multi-channel retailer (Retailintegration.com accessed 16th October 2010)

1. **They recognize the uniqueness of each channel.** Take these differences into consideration at every stage of planning and marketing.
2. **They plan, plan and plan some more**. Planning is critical, from the overall company business plan to individual plans for each channel to integrating channel plans so they make sense.
3. **They review plans regularly**. Conditions can change. A periodic review of plans against actual performance will ensure you're aware of the implications of changing conditions and can respond accordingly.
4. **They consolidate purchasing across channels**. This creates greater purchasing power, often resulting in better pricing from vendors, cost-savings in shipping and transportation, and greater efficiency in consolidating inventory and warehouse operations. 5. **They create a consistent user experience across all channels**. Building a strong brand across channels — from the look and feel of each channel, to product offerings, to the ease of shopping — results in greater loyalty among customers.
Source:www.retailonlineintegration.com, accessed 16th October 2010 [9]

2.4 Multi channel consumer behavior

The consumer follows a number of stages before the decision is made to purchase a certain product, these stages are as defined by Engel et al. (1995) the following: Need recognition, search for information and information processing, pre-purchase alternative evaluation, purchase decision and post-purchase evaluations.

The consumer will use a single or a combination of channels in the different purchasing stages. Multi-channel consumers use at least two channels before they purchase, this can be for example search for information on-line and make the purchase in a physical store. The behavior of utilizing different channels is also known as channel hopping. Schröder and Zaharia (2008) investigated a German multi channel retailer and the consumer behavior.

Two interesting outcomes are worth mentioning, in relation to this paper. The first one is that the majority of the consumers who look for information in one channel also make the purchase in that channel; this outcome is consistent for the on-line and not-online channels. Secondly the consumer behaves different depending on what buying process he is in, this can be product complexity related or linked to the frequency goods are purchased, as this defines the goods familiarity. The retailer needs to understand this behavior to understand and steer the consumer to the channel that is most suitable for that specific consumer's shopping need.

2.5 Internet channel performance

The multi-channel approach will have an effect on the overall company performance. For companies who serve or plan to serve multiple channels need to have a good understanding of the associated benefits and risks that come with multiple channels. The reasons for developing an additional channel to the existing structure needs to include; strengthening the contribution to the company's strategic and financial performance goals. In an article by Wolk and Skiera (2009) the Internet channel performance in relation to existing channels is analyzed.

The main outcome from their study is that the Internet channel improves the strategic and financial performance of the company. In this study two dimensions are defined, these are:

1. The strategic performance relates to the company's market position, that is influenced by the market share, competitiveness, etc

2. The financial performance relates to the sales growth, cost levels and realized profits

The strategic dimension is an indicator of the long-term company position in the market and will drive the financial performance that is measurable in a shorter time span. Adding an additional distribution channel will have an effect on both of the mentioned dimensions.

Research performed by Geyskens (2002) shows that one of the benefits from adding an additional retail channel is creating increased consumer loyalty and that results in strengthening long-term customer relationships. Another important effect from operating multiple channels is that multi channel customers generate higher revenues, this as shown in research by Kumar (2005). Both of them were quoted by Wolk and Skiera (2009) in the earlier mentioned article.

Unfortunately the increased performance is not that simple to measure, as there are a number of other elements, that also need to be positive, first of all the consumers: will they accept to buy from the Internet channel or will they prefer to continue to shop in the traditional store. The Internet channel will have an additional cost, first the initial investment and after the running cost, that includes for example cost for the platform, resources and marketing.

The sales generated by the additional channels, consist out of incremental and/or cannibalization from the existing channels. Cannibalization is not a direct negative performance effect as it depends on the margins generated in the different channels, for example the Internet channel can provide higher margins compared to the bricks (physical stores) channel. Selling on the Internet can also have a negative effect on the other channels due to potential channel conflicts. Retail margins can also come under pressure due to the transparency Internet creates, as prices can be easily compared for the same product or similar products, this can drive competition to act on the pricing and for the consumer to focus more on the price.

Wolk and Skiera (2009) surveyed 142 retail companies that run multiple channels, and have added an Internet channel from Germany, Austria and Switzerland between October 2005 and March 2006. The key outtakes from this research show that:

- Managers are overall positive about the Internet channels
- 70% indicates that the overall company performance increased with the Internet channel added
- 13% indicated the Internet channel performed below their expectations
- 89% of the companies indicate that most of their sales is generated by other channels than the Internet
- 28% experienced channel conflict of some kind
- 39% reports channel cannibalization, this has been in most cases reported as a positive effect

The full statistics analyses can be found in the mentioned article from Wolk and Skiera (2009), their statistics show that both the strategic and financial performance of the company increases after adding a channel. While the strongest effect is on the strategic performance of the company this indicates that the companies added the channel with as aim to become or stay competitive, and maintain or grow their market share.

One important conclusion in the mentioned article, when the added channel has no clear differentiation or added value for the consumer compared to the existing channels it will fail. The consumer is looking for an additional incentive to utilize different channels.

The other very important and interesting outcome is that the level of channel power does not influence the performance of the Internet channel. While in the early days it was the main influence factor for the retailers to decide on adding additional channels. Retailers with low channel power have less advantageous negotiation position towards the manufacture, this can lead to that the margin generated in the Internet channel can be higher but they are not given full access to the range.

This can be translated in the positive effect of cannibalization on margins from sales from the Internet channel. Final recommendation based on this research by Wolk is that retailers should adopt and develop the Internet as it clearly contributes to their overall performance.

2.6 Manufacturer dual-channel and Retail performance

Establishing a direct sales channel operated by the manufacturer has an effect on the performance from the retailer, as the retail improves their services. In research conducted by Yan and Pei (2009) that compares the retail services and profit in the supply chain, before and after the manufacturer adds a direct consumer channel. The retail services they define by all forms of demand-enhancing services that are provided by the retailer, these include the post-purchase services, in-store advertising and promotions, technical and shopping assistance and return services, all of them defining the quality of the total shopping experience.

Their research shows two very important outcomes that give strong argumentation for the manufacturer to add a direct channel. Their two key findings are:

1. The retailers will increase their service performance to counter the effect from the direct manufacturer sales channel, by doing so protecting themselves from being disintermediated
2. Positive effect on the total supply chain cost and performance due to the focus on improving the performance and cost efficiency, additionally due to improved retail services a higher price can be accomplished. Resulting in a more stable price management, and less price erosion.

The analysis setting is explained as follows by Yan and Pei (2009):

They proof their propositions based on the Game theory in a Stackelberg competition setting, the retailer and the manufacturer both consider their own profit while making their respective decisions. The game has a fixed sequence of moves. One key assumption is that the retailer will always have a lower price from the manufacturer than the retailer offers in the direct channel In the first stage the manufacturer considers whether to open a direct channel, for full details and calculations see the paper by Yan and Pei (2009).

The results proof that for a manufacturer it is important to have a direct channel co-existing next to the retail channels, as it drives competition that leads to improvements in the retail services. The direct manufacturer channel has no need to be sales performing, but mainly service performing and setting a standard for the consumer that the retailer will compete with.

The manufacturer has also a potential free-rider challenge, as Vinhas and Anderson (2005) mention in their paper on channel structures and how potential conflicts can drive this structure. When different retailers, that operate in the same channel and approach the same consumer, it is very well possible that the consumer will collect the information in one channel and make the purchase in another. Retailers who understand this can make sure that they sell on price and have other channels invest in the pre-sales services.

2.7 Retail channels summarized

The upcoming of the Internet has changed the retail landscape. At first the pure on-line retailers were able to develop and establish themselves as trusted shops, as the traditional retailers and manufacturers didn't understand or saw the threat of on-line shopping. Till the pure on-line retailers market share started to grow, since then the retailers have embraced the on-line shopping experience. The latest trend is that the retailers are evolving into multi channel retailers. At the same time we see the trend that on-line retailers are adding physical shops to their on-line presence, this would lead to the conclusion that multi channel is the future; only it needs to be executed in a seamless approach in the consumers experience to have the full benefit. The retailer also needs to understand the consumer behavior and preference for the channel depending on what kind of shopping process the consumer is in, for example a new product or regular purchase.

Multi channel retailers perform strategically and financially better than single channel retailers, but to reach this increased performance the different channels need to have a clear differentiation for the shopper. Sales cannibalization is seen often as a negative effect and defined as a risk. Research has shown that cannibalization seems to have in most cases a positive effect on the financial performance.

The author also looked at the overall effect of having the manufacturer compete with retail with a direct channel, research has shown that the overall level of retail services improves; this results in an overall better quality of the consumer shopping experience.

3 Manufacturers and on-line sales

The on-line sales channel development has increased the exposure and availability of branded goods, but has also caused increased channel conflicts and (on-line) price erosion. This is mainly caused by the difference in business models between the physical (brick) and the on-line stores. The latest development is that almost all retailers are setting up a multi channel business model (bricks-and-clicks). As discussed in the previous chapter.

3.1 Manufacturers and Direct sales

Most manufacturers maintain an indirect relation with the consumers, as they sell their products via retailers to consumers. They provide retailers support and services, like brand and product consumer marketing and in most cases and markets the after-sales services under guarantee, as this is a legal requirement.

The manufacturer faces a growing retailer power, the retail landscape in a number of markets has developed into an oligopoly of retailers. These power retailers control not only one market but often some big parts of the retail market in Europe. To mentions some of these retailers are: DSGi, KESA, FNAC, Carrefour, Metro group, Tesco etc. These retailers are more supporting their own store brands than the manufacturer brands, also taking into account the channel conflicts and price erosion, difficulties to get unbiased feedback and reach the consumer. This results in that for the manufacturer they become dependent of the retailer. Without the retailer support it becomes difficult to maintain and develop their brand positioning, price levels and margins and develop their market shares. It is in the retailers' interest to keep the manufacturer selling thru the channels and not direct, to maintain the power.

Manufacturers have started exploring other channels to reach and sell to the consumer, the Internet and the upcoming of e-commerce have fuelled this development. Another key element is how the Internet has changed the power balance, as mentioned earlier the power balance shifted from first the manufacturer, to the retailer, and now the consumer holds the power on where, when and what to buy.

These developments have resulted in that a number of manufacturers opened a direct channel to consumers, and others are considering the same move. The main reason is that, most manufacturers are careful about setting up direct to consumer relations, is the fear of loosing sales and profits, due to the uncertainty in the transition period.

The direct sales channel is in most cases established by manufacturers next to the existing channels (see Figure 7), as an additional sales channel. By adding the channel the channel conflicts are likely to increase as retail experiences it as new threat to their operations and business results, like they have in the early days of e-commerce experienced with the pure on-line retailers (clicks).

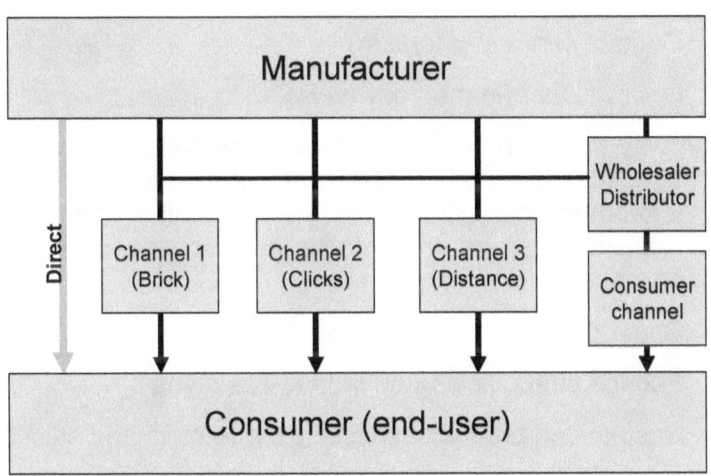

Figure 7 - Channel structure with a direct channel

Not all manufacturers have chosen the same approach for when to establish the direct on-line to consumer sales channel. Some manufacturers established their direct channel in the early days of on-line sales, while some are still undecided what strategy to implement. Till early 2000 the early adopters had as benefit that the retailers didn't see a treat from the on-line sales channel, as they didn't expect consumers to buy on-line.

Two of the most noticeable early adopters were: Dell and Sony, they both pursued a different strategy, as for Dell it was their only way to enter the market and sell direct to consumers and developed it into their core sales channel. Sony top management saw at the end of the nineties the opportunity to add the direct to consumer sales channel, this they decided to create under the "SonyStyle" brand.

Not all brands decided to explore the on-line channel as their first direct to consumer sales channel, other examples for selling direct to consumers are via:

- Flagship stores
- Shop in shop
- Outlet stores
- Catalogues
- Contact centres (phone in)
- Door to Door (in the early days)

Another way that manufacturers develop their direct sales is thru differentiate the product ranges that are marketed to the consumer compared to what is sold via the retail channel. These ranges consist often of low profile and service (after-sales) oriented products, like:

- Spare parts, accessories and consumables
- Service offers, like extended service plans
- Customized products, specially made or limited editions
- Out of range products, factory outlet styles

None of these product groups provide a real opportunity for the manufacturer to test and develop their direct to consumer sales channel, the direct marketing experience and to develop closer consumer relations for their core products.

Recently during Q2/Q3 2010, a number of apparel brands have announced to start an on line direct sales channel or to extend it to other regions, some examples are:

- H&M, opened their first on-line store as published in the Internetretailing.net [11] at the 17th of September 2010:

"Fashion retailer H&M's online store is now open for UK business"

- Zara, started in September 2010 with on-line sales, as stated in the FT.com (2010) [12]: "The long-awaited roll-out of Zara's transactional website will begin in Spain, the UK, Portugal, Italy, Germany and France – six countries that are among the most important of the company's 76 markets." Their CEO commented: "For us, now is the right time to go online."

- GAP, in the USA selling for a number of years on-line, now expanding into other markets as stated on businessweek.com (2010) [10]: "The company said it expects international and online sales to account for 25 percent of its revenue by fiscal 2013. In 2009, those areas made up 12 percent of revenue."

One of the reasons is that the apparel industry has become more active on-line is that the on-line presentation of clothes and accessories have dramatically increased in the recent years and in combination with the availability of fast Internet. Interesting to mention is one of the first on-line shop failures. This was an on-line shop that created a very sophisticated process to sell and present clothes on-line, by using avatars and 3d-models. Unfortunately they had not taken into account the Internet speed available to their targeted consumer group at that time. This company was Boo.com and they had one of the biggest cash burn rates of the late 90's early 2000's, and became an example of the Internet bubble. For further reading see the on-line article [8] on the Boo.com case.

The on-line market for manufacturers' in-direct sales and direct sales continuous to grow rapidly, this is confirmed by the next extract from an article as published on Internetretailing.net [7] based on a report by Forrester (2010):

"Nearly two-thirds of manufacturer site visitors say they seek product information, suggesting that the sites should focus on detailed product information, the report says. It goes on to say that 45% of manufacturer site visitors who later made a purchase did so online from other retailers. Another 17% of consumers bought the product from the manufacturer directly."

Key outtakes are that the importance for the manufacturer websites is of high importance for the consumer, as 45% bought goods after visiting. 17% of the consumer even bought directly from the manufacturer, keeping in mind that not all the manufacturers have direct sales shops, this shows a great potential for the manufacturers and the consumer appetite to buy branded goods directly from the manufacturer.

In the next chapter the question about why selling direct to the consumer will be further explored.

3.2 Rational for direct sales to consumers

For many manufacturers there are a number of internal and external challenges or argumentations that build the rational for why the company should sell direct to consumers. In this paragraph the "why" will be discussed.

3.2.1 *Why direct sales to consumers?*

Taking into account the risk of channel conflicts, the shift in the channel power and the uncertainty about future profits, and in most cases an internal push back on going direct. What is the rational behind going online, besides that your competitors are doing it, this is a key question to be answered, and how to get the support from the management and the different stakeholders in the organization.

For clarification the direct sales channel that is in focus, are not the direct sales channels as used by some manufacturers by using party, event or temporary sales set-ups. The direct sales channel that is in focus is the manufacturer controlled direct sales channel, and is not temporary of nature.

Based on feedback from several manufacturers, the professional survey and literature, there are a few key reasons mentioned by manufacturers to go direct. Each of them will be explored in more detail in this chapter. To start with five rationales that are taken from an article about the car industry, direct sales and building consumer relations by Parment (2008), these are:

1. Control and standardization
2. Marketing reasons, disintermediation
3. Creating a standard
4. Market tentacles

5. Overcapacity, safety valve

Additional the following are often mentioned in relation to online sales:

6. Oligopoly
7. Entering new markets
8. Direct consumer interaction
9. Establishing price points
10. Increasing profits
11. Consumer demand

Based on the professional survey conducted for this thesis the top 3 reasons for selling direct to consumers given are:

1. Marketing, more control and building the brand experience
2. Consumer demand, the consumer expects to buy direct from the manufacturer
3. Profit, overall improvement, profitable sales to consumers

The rationale for the benefits or reasons for selling direct to consumers are different for each manufacture due to their products, brand and market situation. Below are the most common relevant reasons listed with a short explanation of why that can be used for the consideration or motivation of direct sales.

1   Control and standardization
   • Manufacturers loose control on the quality of the product display and product knowledge as soon as the product is sold to the retailer, as they have their own staff and processes. Only way to maintain such control for a manufacturer is to provide bonuses or place their own staff in the stores, this is often too expensive or not allowed.
2   Marketing reasons, disintermediation
   • The product ranging, display and the supporting materials develop a strong brand specific experience, that strengthens the brand and the values it want to represent. This experience is very difficult to control with retailers as the products are displayed in a multi brand setting, and each brand has their own requirements and

wishes. By having it in own control the manufacturer can provide a consistent brand message from pre-sales, during sales and after sales.

- Retailer own brand has in many products groups established their own position and often directly competing with the manufacturer brands, while in many cases the retailer will prefer their own brand over the manufacturer brand to position and sell. As stated by Juhl et al. (2006): "store brands are seen a strategic weapon, because they offer the retailer more control" and "the retailer typically obtains higher profit margins on the store brands" this explains partly their preference over manufacturer brands, and the challenge to bring the brand message to the shop floor.
- By selling direct it allows the manufacturer to take control of the brand, the marketing message and experience towards the consumer, this is possible by removing the retailer interaction.

3 Creating a standard

- Directly linked to first and second points, as manufacturer they want to set a standard of how their products can be displayed, what information needs to be available and what services to provide the consumer with all the knowledge and experience needed. This to be established by creating on-line or physical flag-ship stores that function as examples of the standard and often to test new concepts. The sales function is important for measuring the conversion and related metrics.

4 Market tentacles

- By having their own sales environment the manufacturer can learn about retailing, and get to know better their markets. The interaction with consumer provides unbiased feedback, this they can use to improve their marketing and sales material, and even can support better product development.

5 Overcapacity, safety valve

- This is less valid for premium brands, but manufacturers prefer to control their overstock and how this positioned in the market, as selling out of goods below market value can damage the brand value and sales margins for a long time. By taking this sales in own control it can be planned and managed well how it is distributed and priced into the market, by doing so avoiding retail interactions.

6 Oligopoly
- In many markets only a handful of retailers control the market, and by having this oligopoly, each of them have strong purchasing power to put demands on the manufacturer, else they will just not list their products. To show these retailers that as manufacturer there are new ways to reach the consumer the direct road can be used to find better ways of cooperation, resulting in partnerships with a limited number of retailers that do support the brand values.

7 Entering new markets
- The on-line channel enables a direct access to a new market, without having to establish a retail distribution the products become accessible for a whole market (country). Keeping in mind that sales growth will only be reached with sufficient brand awareness and traffic to the sites, these are to be taken into consideration in the market entry strategy.

8 Direct consumer interaction
- By having direct interaction with consumers, it enables the manufacturer to get unfiltered and unbiased feedback from the consumer, and enables measurement of their behavior and needs. This also creates great opportunities for future targeting and consumer marketing related activities, as in most cases the retailers maintains this information In their records, and the manufacturer only gets back in touch with the consumer when they have a problem under warranty.

9 Establishing price points
- The manufacturer can make a clear communication on what they see as the market price points for each product offer, this with or without added services. The retailers and consumers can compare the different price offers and the manufacturer price would be the guidance for the market price. Some manufacturers also use their on-line store to set a higher price than the real market price with as purpose to give the retailers a possibility to sell underneath that price, by doing so having less price erosion. In this case volume or profit in the direct sales channel is not of importance for the manufacturer.

10 Increasing profits
- The direct sales channel for manufacturers has the potential to increase profits for the manufacturer, the opportunity is to be found in two different areas:
  a. Reaching a new consumer group, this leading to additional sales that will contribute directly to the bottom line, this consumer group is mainly attracted by the on-line offer and attracted by the brand, but were before not able to find the products at the retailers, due to availability or the retailers provided arguments to make them decided to purchase another brand, like the store brand.
  b. Cannibalization from the retail channel, in most cases the direct sales channel will have a higher profitability for the manufacturer than the retail channel sales, as all margin generated will be kept in the books of the manufacturer, this additional income is mainly the retail margin and from cost savings from not having to pay the retailer for marketing and trainings. This should be sufficient to cover the additional cost of the direct sales and create additional profit for the manufacturer.
- The profits will only be achieved if there is certain volume reached to cover the fixed cost of the sales platform, the cost for direct consumer marketing, etc. Finally there is also a positive cash-flow effect as the payments are received 30 – 90 days in advance from retailers.

11 Consumer demand
- The consumer shows that it is willing to buy direct from the manufacturer, as this is a trusted source, and today they almost expect that they can buy directly all products from any websites, as this has become common practice for all retailers and retailer brands. This is not yet common practice on the manufacturer sites, even though their products are available on the Internet via retail sites. The consumer demand can be easily analyzed by having a survey out on the brand sites asking and ask the consumer feedback.
- Power shift to the consumer, as earlier mentioned, the consumer holds the power and has taken it over from the retailer, the consumer wants the control and freedom to buy the product that they are looking for from a trusted

source. They use the Internet to find all the information they need to make such buying decision.

Most of the above arguments are valid for all different company size manufacturers. The smaller manufacturers that operate in a niche market can enter the market place with their product via on-line sales. By using on-line sales they can reach a wider audience and reach easier their target group, then going via retail in a more cost efficient way, of course if their products are fit for on-line sales.

3.2.2   Arguments against direct sales

As there are many arguments that are in favor of selling direct to consumers there are also a number of arguments and areas that need to be assessed before starting direct sales operations. These arguments can be mainly split between external and internal reasons.

External reasons are mainly the ones connected to retailers, the manufacturer's customer, and fear of loss of sales. The retailers will claim that the manufacturer will cannibalize from the existing retailers sales. This potentially will result in channel conflicts and the retailer will most probably use his channel power to influence the manufacturer. The retailer has a number of tools that they can use that can potentially harm the manufacturer sales or at least presence on the shop floor. The key measures a retailer can take, as response to the manufacturer direct sales are:

- Reducing orders, order more from and focus more on other manufacturers
- Reducing floor space, reducing the number of spots on the shop floor or placing the products in less prominent spots
- De-listing the manufacturer, this is the most radical decision a retailer can make is to totally stop ordering from a certain manufacturer.
  - On www.direct2consumeronline.com [16], website operated by Digital River, they list the benefits and concerns of going direct, the channel conflict is disproved being a concern based on research carried out by Jupiter with manufacturers that sell direct.

o This indicates, despite it is the biggest internal fear from the manufacturer, the retailers seems to appreciate the relationship and branded products. It also shows that the manufacturers that went direct have taken the right measures to mitigate any conflict and have good relationship management.

A key outtake is that it is clear that each manufacturer indicates other effects, keeping in mind that the information is based on a limited response group, but overall it shows there is none or a positive effect.

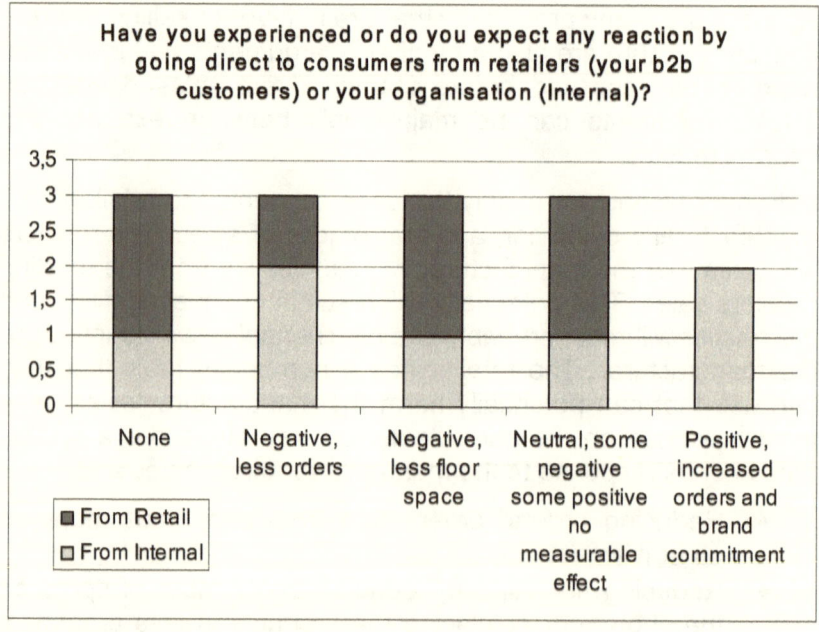

Figure 8 - Retail reaction from retail (Professional survey)

Some comments as posted in the professional survey, both coming from experienced manufacturers with active direct sales to consumers:

"Genuine fear from the internal sales organization"

"Most of the push back is internal. The external push back is largely self inflicted (badly managed distribution policy)"

These indicate that there is mainly an internal fear and push back, this is not reflected in the earlier mentioned research.

In the professional survey it was also asked, if any had experienced any negative effect from retail, what measures the manufacturer decided to take. The measures taken to mitigate the conflicts were not disclosed in detail by the manufacturers that been part of the survey or direct talks. From different researches it shows that the retailers negative effect is very limited to none, it shows in most cases even a positive effect.

Figure 8 on the previous page shows that most manufacturers experience a positive retail effect from selling direct to consumers. This can be experienced by more orders and stronger commitment to the brand and its display by retailers.

The consumer experience, if not well executed or if the organization is not ready for selling direct to consumers can result in a negative experience and resulting in brand devaluation. If the manufacturer feels it is not able to support the consumer shopping experience, this can result in the strongest arguments against direct sales. The manufacturer can fix this by a total process review and deploying best practices from retail (B2C).

The impact on the different value chain activities is a good way to understand the change in the go-to-market strategy for the manufacturer. The value chain linked to the Internet strategy will have additional functions that are needed to support the consumer business compared to the existing business to business model. As base model the generic value chain model (Porter, 1985) see Figure 9 is a good starting point. Most of the activities will need to be analyzed to understand the impact of the chosen strategy, as most of the processes and services are set-up for business to business, these need to be checked on how they are supporting business to consumers.

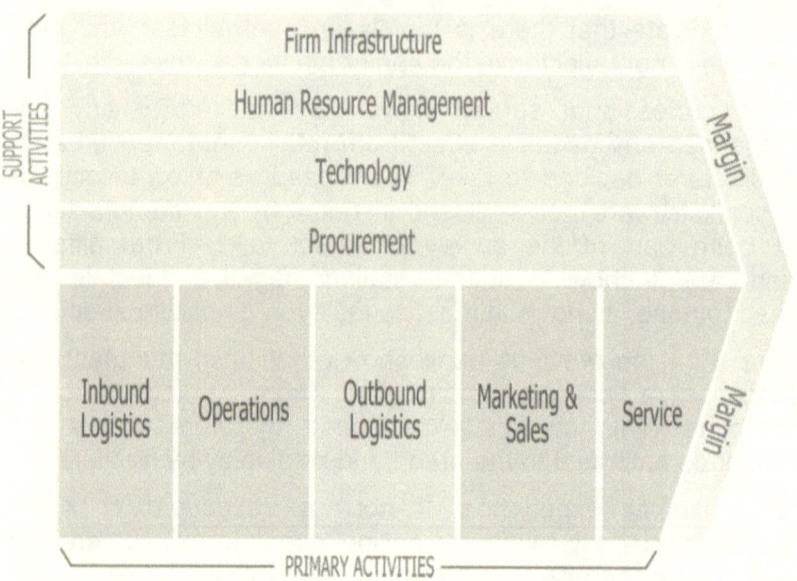

Figure 9 - Visualization for Porter's Value Chain (Dinesh Pratap Singh)

Areas that will be mainly affected or need to change are the activities that are needed to support the different sales to consumer processes. As an example we take the strategy that has the biggest impact on the organization, the direct consumer on-line sales strategy by the manufacturer.

Activities that need to be developed are the ones that will differ when dealing directly with consumers compared to dealing with business, these can be listed as below and this list is not covering all areas that need attention, as these will differ by business model:

- Consumers sales, instead of a limited number of known customers (retail) many "anonymous" consumers
- Consumer service (contact centers)
- Online transactional consumer website that is conversion driving
- Payment and fraud checking services
- Consumer fulfillment, like single drops and home delivery and installation
- Return and exchange processes
- Consumer (direct) marketing
- Etc…

Most of these processes are linked to delivering consumer service in a convenience way in low volume too many individuals, not servicing big orders and a limited group of known customers. The challenge for the organization is to have next to the B2B processes have specialized B2C processes that are mainly enabled by the Internet.

By setting up the B2C business model the organization should analyze what activities should be shared and what activities should be separated for reaching synergies, but also avoiding negative influence from the core business. Markides and Charitou (2004) analyzed the effect of developing two different business models in a integrated or disintegrated way. Their research shows that "simultaneously running two business models that inherent conflicts and market dissimilarities is extremely difficult to manage and likely to fail".

In Figure 10 the key areas are listed that the surveyed professionals indicated as the major biggest organizational challenges when going to sell direct.

Figure 10 - Organizational challenges (Professional survey)

Marketing is listed as the biggest challenge; one of the key reasons is that the marketing approach between B2B and B2C is different. The marketing focus was before direct sales focused on the brand building, and conversion in the retail stores. By changing to direct sales the marketing effort is focusing on traffic that will convert in the Brand shop. The manufacturer brand positioning and direct consumer relation is very important to drive the desired result.

These values need to be part of the marketing mix and in how the consumer will affiliate themselves with the brand and the store. Within the execution plan and briefing of the marketing and brand teams this needs to be covered.

Consumer direct marketing, activation and retention activities are with most manufacturers not well developed. To establish this CRM programs are to be developed and resulting in one single view of the consumer when he or she is contacting the company.

The sales channel strategy will need to be consistent and balanced to optimize the sales across the different channels. By having a holistic approach it will avoid channel conflicts or mitigate the risk from adding the direct channel. Important element of the sales strategy is the strategic pricing, first to set the prices and after to monitor the real market prices. Especially in the European market with the open borders and Internet, pricing differences are transparent for the consumer. To successfully implement a direct channel the pricing, service and channel structure will need to be harmonized and well controlled.

The pricing of products that are sold on-line need to be seen as new approach to pricing, as Internet provides different mechanics for tracking consumer behavior and by doing so offering products and services that meet the needs of that consumer. Yield management needs a different approach than selling to retail, as Marmorstein et al. (2003) puts it: "Yield Management on the Internet should not be viewed merely as faster, cheaper pricing tactic, but rather as new business strategy that capitalizes on all elements of the marketing mix." They also comment on the advantage of providing personalized bundles: "Companies can monitor individual customer demand and respond with tailored products and services."

To enable efficient and sophisticated sales methods to consumers the on-line sales platform needs to be well defined and selected as each business has it own specific requirements. To discuss all the different on-line sales platform in detail are not within scope of this paper.

Key decision and differentiation that need to be taken into consideration are:

- Partial of fully outsourced solution, or run all in house
- Level of integration to current organizational set-up
- Separate business unit, or part of the established organization and shared resources
- Specific requirements for manufacturing and ware-housing

To support the on-line business model all the needed resources and positions will need to be well defined for this the Human Resource Management function will need to be involved.

3.2.3 Arguments and Readiness summarized

Internal versus external argumentation differs for selling direct or not, before a manufacturer starts to sell the internal organization is expecting a lot of issues with the channel partners (customers), based on the research this seems not to be the case. This internal push back for going direct is best managed by analyzing the channel and making sure that there is clear channel and distribution strategy in place.

The organizational readiness can be an area of concern, as the consumer expects the best service and brand experience, this need to be supported by the organization.

Any of the manufacturers will have to make their own balance between the positive and negative elements for going direct. The brand element is often mentioned as one of the key drivers behind direct sales. The brand is important as it is the biggest differentiator for the manufacturer and it is also presents the manufacturer products to the consumer. For this reason the brand dimension in relation to direct sales will be further explored in the next part.

3.3 Direct sales and Existing Brands on-line

The Internet channel strategy is of paramount importance for the manufacturer to establish the direct to consumer channel. For the consumer the direct sales channel is the only interface that they have towards the manufacturer, besides going through the retailers. The manufacturers that have established channels to consumers pursue these for different reasons and have developed different strategies on how to sell their goods to consumers and how to or not to cooperate with retailers. In two articles about Internet channel strategies by Lee et al. (2001) and by Choi et al. (2010), they have investigated a number of manufacturer approaches to on-line sales, and what channel strategies can be applied to avoid channel conflicts or to make sure that the added direct channel has the optimal contribution to the company results. Web appropriateness as mentioned earlier plays an important role in defining the channel strategy and in managing the channel conflict risk.

First we look at the channel strategies approach as defined by Lee, and after the approach by Choi.

3.3.1 Internet Channel Strategies as defined by Lee et al.

Lee et al. (2001) identified the following five channel conflict management strategies based on twenty manufacturer cases that are operating successfully direct sales:

1. Differentiation Strategy (Based on: Market or Product differentiation)
2. Intermediary support Strategy
3. Conflict avoidance Strategy
4. Channel absorption Strategy
5. Compromising Strategy (Based on: Information or Profit sharing)

The strategies are classified as shown in Figure 11, each strategy is placed in one of the 5 quadrants from the conflict management model as shown in Figure 12. This general conflict management model was developed by Rahim (2000).

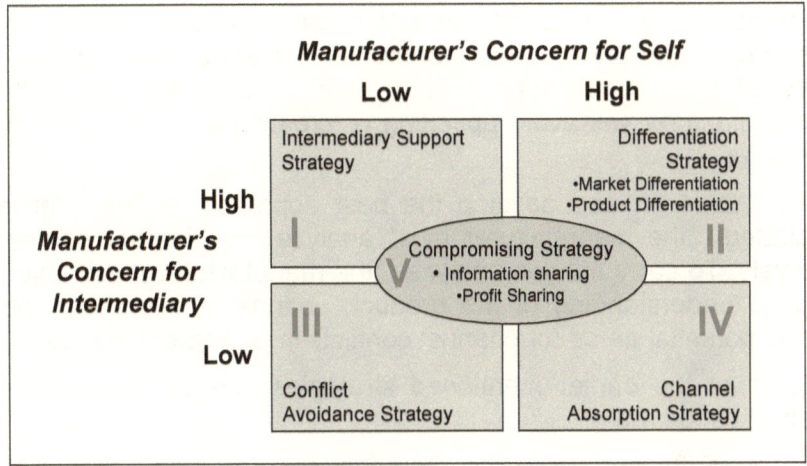

Figure 11 - Conflict management strategies (Lee et al., 2003)

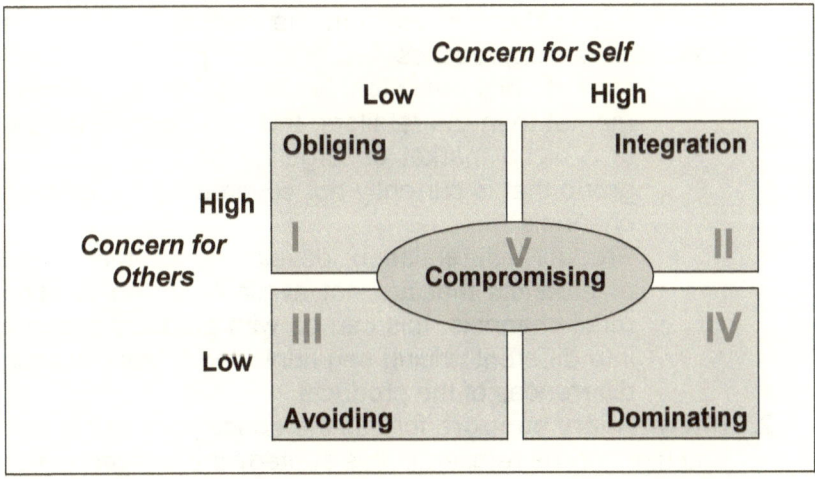

Figure 12 - Conflict management model (Rahim, 2000)

The model and its dimensions can be explained as follows; it consist out of 2 concern dimensions (self and others) and five strategies (obliging, integration, avoiding, dominating and compromising).

The dimension concern defines how much the manufacturer cares for the other party in most cases the retailer. High concern for self indicates that the manufacturers mainly care for themselves and that the retailers come second in defining the strategic choices for the manufacturer on-line sales strategy. When the manufacturer has a high concern for others the manufacturer will avoid upsetting or creating a conflict with the retailer.

To decide on and develop the best approach for the Internet strategy, the manufacturer must analyze the different concern levels. To carry out this analyzes the manufacturer must have a good understanding of the product, channel and brand power and potential areas for channel conflicts in pricing or services.

Each of the earlier mentioned strategies can be explained in short as follows:

1. **Differentiation**: the manufacturer has high concern for others and self, they will try to avoid competing directly in the same space as the retailer, this will also result in avoiding cannibalization of the channels , this by differentiating themselves from the retailer, this can be done with two approaches
   - Market differentiation: entering in a different market than the retailers, this can be for example in a niche market or targeting another customer group that is currently not covered by the existing channels
   - Product differentiation; developing another range of products that are not available in the existing retail channels, this can be with products that are in a different pricing segment, due to specification differences of the products
2. **Intermediary support**: for this the concern for self is low, and high for the retailer, in this strategy the retailer avoids any conflict with the retailer, and supports the retailer with their on-line strategy, examples of this approach are shop locators, that shows where the closest dealer can be found or direct links to the website from the retailers where the products can be bought, the manufacturer is not selling any products direct to the consumer.
3. **Conflict avoidance**: as in the intermediary support the concern for self is low and for others is high, the difference in this strategy is that the manufacturer will have shop locators and all refers to the retailer for example with special retail promotions, but they have

created within the main site also some direct sales options that are not very clearly available, or they have established some shadow sites where they have direct sales, normally this practice will be discovered sooner or later by retail, it can be an accepted tactic to test products or new channels.

4. **Channel absorption**: for this strategy the manufacturer has a high concern of self, and low for the retailers, the manufacturer channel strategy is to take ownership of the channel, in the extreme case of this strategy the products will only be sold on the Internet by the manufacturer, if any previous relations with retail existed, then these will be discontinued. Dell has followed this strategy from the beginning for the Internet channel.

5. **Compromising strategy**: the aim of this strategy is to have a close cooperation between retailers and manufacturers, by doing so creating a compromise on the channel usage, and explore how to gain mutual benefits, these are to be found in two areas that the compromising strategy by can be split by:

    ▪ Information sharing: consumer information that is collected from the on-line channel, this information is shared between the partners, for example the email addresses, by doing so reaching together more consumers. Some manufacturers provide the retailers with support for their websites so they can improve the conversion, from this they share back shopper behavior to the manufacturer.

    ▪ Profit sharing: the manufacturer will share profits generated by the on-line channel, a number of mechanics are known on how to share profits back with the retailer, some examples: based on zip code where the product was delivered, the origin from the consumer information, general sharing with all retailers.

3.3.2 Internet Channel Strategies as defined by Choi et al.

The Internet channel strategic framework hat Choi et al. published in 2009 is based on two factors, the channel conflict and the web appropriateness. For this they analyzed sixty-three Korean firms across thirteen industries. See

Appendix 4 for the outcome and placement of the companies they researched in the four clusters that Choi et al. (2009) defined in his strategic framework. The web appropriateness factors are discussed in paragraph 2.2.

The channel conflict factor is driven by a number of elements, Choi et al. (2009) based their analysis on the following six elements and their degree of influence:

1. Degree of Competition: among channels within an industry and sensitivity to customers' requirement
2. Degree of Concentrated industry structure: distribution of sales and production within an industry
3. Degree of Customer switching cost: customer's cost and effort required to switch from one product to another
4. Degree of Irreplaceability: to which the partner and the value received are irreplaceable
5. Degree of Power sources strength: strength of available power sources
6. Degree ofChannel dependence: dependence of one channel member upon another

The strategic framework is based on the two above mentioned factors that Choi et al. (2009) placed along the axis by doing so creating four clusters. For each of the clusters he developed a go-to market strategy, the framework is shown in Figure 13.

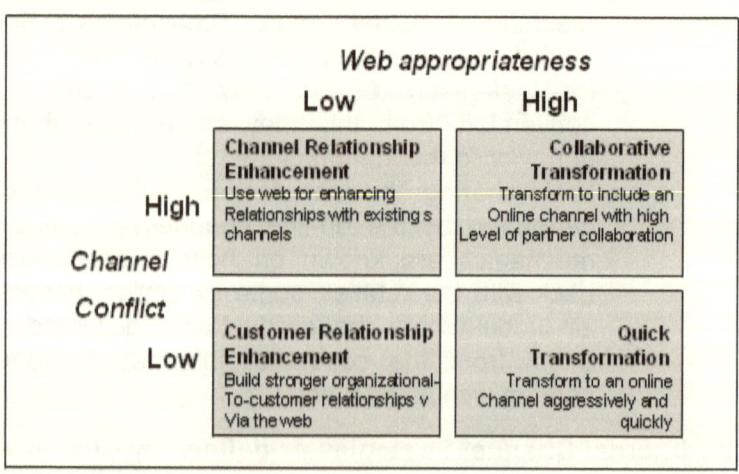

Figure 13 - Internet channel framework, four web usage strategies (Choi et al.)

The four Internet channel strategies that Choi et al.(2009) proposes are presented in Figure 14 on the next page. It shows the different product/service (solid line) flow and information (dotted line) flow between the manufacturer, sales channel and customer.

1. Channel Relationship Enhancement, when a high channel conflict and low web appropriateness
2. Customer Relationship Enhancement, when a low channel conflict and low web appropriateness
3. Collaborative Transformation, when a high channel conflict and web appropriateness
4. Quick transformation, when low channel conflict and high web appropriateness

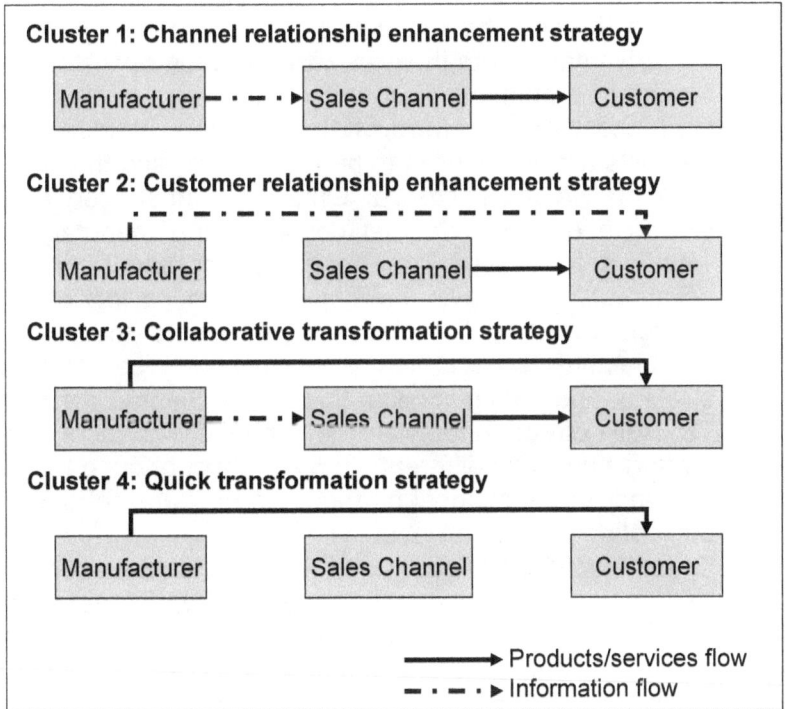

Figure 14 - Web usage strategies (Choi et al.)

Each of the proposed strategies have a specific way to market and cooperation with the channel partners or the customer (the customer as the end-user/consumer), each can be explained in short as follows:

1. **Channel Relationship Enhancement**: This approach focuses on building relationships with existing off-line sales channels, for two reasons: the high channel conflict will require a lot of attention and management, and secondly their products are not will suited for on-line sales. By supporting the existing off-line channels in selling to the customer will be the most successful approach. The on-line support can for example include shop locators on the manufacturer website, only most of the focus will be on the physical stores.

2. **Customer Relationship Enhancement**: Focus on building relation with the actual user of the product, through the brand, and this can be accomplished by providing intensive and rich product information on the manufacturer web, but the product sales and fulfillment will be through the channel partner. The manufacturer can drive sales from the web with web promotions or with for example printable discount codes.

3. **Collaborative Transformation**: The manufacturer products are very well fit to be sold on-line and thus have great on-line sales potential. Only they also are very likely to cause a major channel conflict if the manufacturer would sell direct. The manufacturer must find a collaboration to have the benefits from selling on-line without upsetting the channel partners to much. The manufacturer best option is to have a clear Internet strategy and communicates this to his channel partners. To sell direct and via the channel partners, the manufacturer can differentiate his product offering for on-line and for the channel partners, so they are not directly competing on product level.

4. **Quick transformation**: Manufacturers that are operating with products that have high web appropriateness and are not facing high channel conflicts when they would sell direct. For these manufacturers it is advised to make a quick set-up to sell directly to the consumer, as they get the full control on the brand and can control the whole selling process. This approach should also result in protection of margins, depending on the initial costs and direct marketing this approach should result in better net results. The manufacturer must keep in mind that selling

direct with consumer requires different skill sets and they will face another competitive environment.

The proposed Internet strategies by Choi et al.(2009) support and encourages to use the Internet for providing complete information about the products and services. Additionally the web can be used to increase the customer satisfaction by providing self-service. To use the channel also for direct sales is only advised for the collaborative and quick transformation cluster. Choi et al. (2001) study of sixty-three companies, in thirteen industries (see for details Appendix 4), reveals that related industries are to be found in the same cluster. This implies that most manufacturers are following the same strategy as the industry they are part of. Some exceptions are to be seen and these are mainly related to the (potential) channel conflict management, as not all manufacturers have the same channel power, so some can be more aggressive in their direct sales ambitions than others in the same industry.

The potential channel conflict is also depending on the size of the market and the ambition of shares of that market the manufacturer is competing for. Vinhas and Anderson (2005) touch on this point: "Collision occurs when channel types pursue the same prospects, especially when they present the same offerings. This is why suppliers limit their use of concurrent channels when going to low-growth markets. Here, channel types have fewer opportunities to make the sales that are necessary to cover their investments".

Thus, they compete more fiercely and approach the same customers". Coelho and Easingwood (2008) observed the same about market size in their research, that the smaller and fast growing markets are less likely to provide enough resources to justify a multi channel strategy. In the same research Coelho and Easingwood (2008) observed that companies with a wider range are making more extensive use of multi channel strategy. The logic behind is that when companies can build and share the resources needed for the multi channel set-up with more products it will provide them with economies of scale, and by doing so create a higher profit for the company.

The manufacturer needs to understand and assess all potential areas that can cause a channel conflict or influence the multi channel set-up know prior to deciding on the Internet strategy.

For the identified conflict areas a plan should be made how to mitigate the risk if these could have a negative effect on the future company performance.

For this purpose the Decision-making framework to solve a channel conflict can be applied as defined by Bucklin (1997).

To understand the importance of the channel it is important to measure the future profitability that is at risk. The advised way to measure the risk is by calculating the net present value of the expected cash flow after having added the direct channel, and comparing the results with business as today with expected growth of volumes and cost. By making these calculations the financial impact on the company can be easily analyzed and decided on what actions are needed.

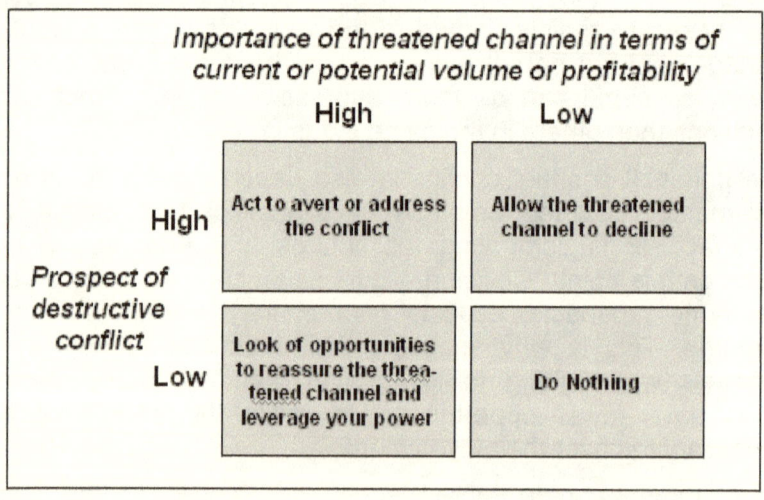

Figure 15 - Decision making framework (Bucklin)

When the financial impact is low no actions are needed, actions can be do nothing or let the channel decline (positive cannibalization). When the financial risk is high actions need to be defined to mitigate the risk, or change the strategy.

3.3.3 Summary Internet strategies

The strategies that Lee and Choi propose are both good guidance on how to deal with the Internet channel, and what the strategic choices are for a manufacturer to enter the direct sales channel. In both Internet strategy approaches the channel conflict element is present. The differentiation between the 2 models is to be found in the other factor, the web appropriateness and the concern for self or the other. Both these factors can be related back to Internet channel power created by the product, or by the brand.

The Internet strategy decision is influenced by additional factors that need to be taken into account, an important one is the market size, another competition behavior that also changes by changing distribution structure and the organizational readiness to sell on-line. To understand the effect on the organization it is advised to calculate the effect on the future financial performance by channel, and if needed define a plan to mitigate potential negative effects.

One shortcoming of the mentioned strategies is that they do not take into account or reflect on the value of the return flow of information directly from the consumer back into the organization. This information flow normally ends at the retailer and only a limited or biased feedback reaches the manufacturer. This information can contain information that can be of high value, like: satisfaction and experience with the products, and consumer details. This information can be used for direct marketing or product improvement.

3.4 The Brand and Direct sales

The manufacturer brand is one of the most important assets for the manufacturer to reach the consumer. The brand is often the only visible manufacturer expression that the consumer recognizes and has an affiliation with.

Within the arguments of why going direct the brand is often mentioned as one of the key arguments, as this is the only online experience where the manufacturer has full control on how the products and brand are presented and priced.

The importance of the brand and the reason for direct sales can be split in two approaches:

- The brand is to support the direct sales channel
- The direct sales channel will support the brand

Taking the first approach the brand is to support the direct channel; the manufacturer pursues a channel strategy with a higher concern for their own concerns. To execute on these strategies the manufacturer will deploy a go-to-market strategy that will be strongly supported by the brand.

This approach needs a strong consumer brand that is already well positioned in the market place. The direct shop will need to have the trust and traffic from consumers to reach sales volumes. The brand is clearly an enabler for creating the consumer experience. The manufacturers who maintain such strong brands in general also hold the power in the channel. This puts them in a very strong position to establish the direct channel, and as their brand are in general also in high demands by consumers. Reflecting back on who holds the true channel power and the power shift that has recently occurred mainly caused by the Internet is that the consumer holds the power, and they decide what brand they buy and where they buy it. This new power balance allows the manufacturer to connect directly with the consumer. The retailer has less power to control the consumer and the manufacturer can utilize this strong position of the brand to establish the direct sales channel, with little concern about the retailers. They can make this work as the retailer needs the branded products in their shop as the consumer expects it there. This puts the manufacturer in a comfortable position when setting up the direct channel, as they have little to worry about the channel conflict.

The second approach is that the direct sales channel will support building the brand. Many manufacturers don't have control on how the products are presented by retail. The retail pricing they cannot set as this is forbidden by the European competition laws, it is only possible to provide suggested retail prices. For manufacturers opening a direct channel gives them the benefit of having a sales channel that is fully in their control. This control enables them to interact with the consumers and created the branded experience that brand should represent.

The direct interaction also enables to be in direct contact with the consumers that have an interest in that brand. This direct interaction can be used to collect more information about the consumer group that shows interest in the brand and its products. The data collection includes personal and often product data; for example the e-email addresses and the product model the consumers owns. This information can be used for targeted direct marketing campaigns. By receiving the information directly removes the need to receive this information from retailers. The retailers are considered to create bias on how the brand is being positioned and the experience that is created. In Figure 16 the flow of consumer information is explained in a graphical way.

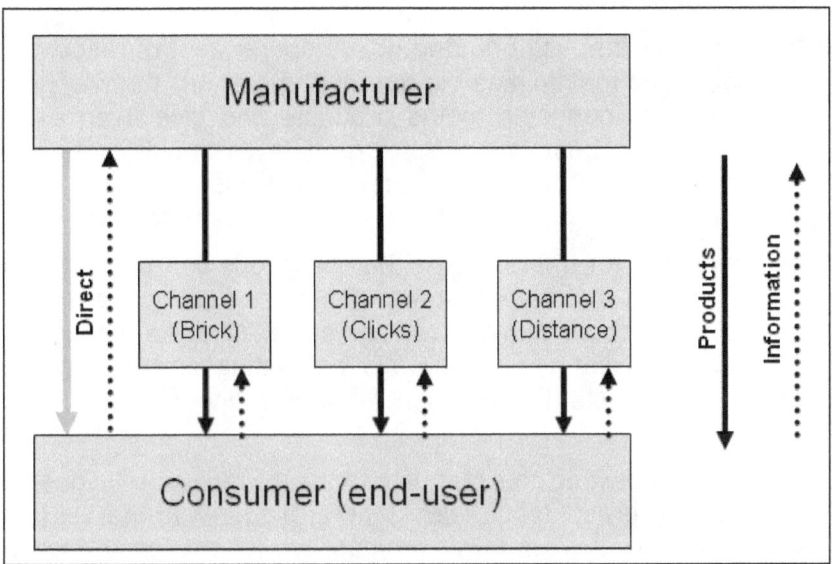

Figure 16 - Direct information flow

The retailers are not caring for one specific brand at the point of sales, as many of them work with a number of brands, this mix of brands on the floor is in most cases creating a negative experience for a single brand, due to lack of focus and knowledge. Nowadays some retailers have a strong preference to build their own brand, for this purpose they use the manufacturer brands to build their retail brand. This practice is often creating a channel conflict between the manufacturer and retailer as the retailers does not create the exposure as agreed. Manufacturers who want to strengthen their brand by opening their own direct channel need to be very careful on what channel strategy they choose. The main reason to be careful is due to the limited brand and channel power most of the manufacturers have compared to the retailers who hold more channel power.

One other dimension is when the brand is reasonable unknown the product might be the key differentiator. The manufacturer can utilize the direct channel to build distribution for the product.

This leads to the question what do consumers expect for branded experience in (single) brand stores, what makes the consumer visit a brand store and how do manufacturers live up to the expectations.

3.4.1 The in-store branded experience

Manufacturers that sell branded goods spend a lot of resources on building and maintaining the brand. The brand is the way how the consumers connects to the products and give it an extra experience and trust layer; this brand layer should create a premium for the product. This premium is also creating extra value (higher sales price) for the retailer and manufacturer.

The advantage for the retailer is that the goods can be sold with a premium and that the consumer has more trust in the quality and service support, this makes it an easier sale. As mentioned earlier the retailers are not always presenting and pricing the brand and products that the manufacturer in line with the brand guidelines.

The tension between the manufacturer and retailer relationship on shop floor presentation is in general bigger with the volume retailers as they have a lower profitability and are less eager to comply, compared to the premium retailers they normally do comply with the brand guidelines, as explained by Parment (2008).

For this purpose the manufacturer builds often into their agreements conditions related to the product display and promotion. The content of the in store display and support for promotions are often provided by the manufacturer. The retailer is not always allowing a too high level of brand influence in their store as they want to maintain their own retail brand experience in store.

To find a good balance and support between the manufacturer and retailer and have common goals that are based on a long term relationships and not just focused on discounts and short term promotions. To manage this relation the trade marketing function was established to be the intermediary between brand, marketing and sales teams and the retailer to build profitable business together, and making sure that the brands and products are presented to create the best possible brand experience.

Dupuis and Tissler-Desbordes (1996) reviewed different definitions for the Trade Marketing function, based on the existing ones, they proposed a new definition: "a methodical procedure carried out by jointly by suppliers and retailers, whose objective it is better serve the customers' needs and expectations, increase profitability and competitive position while taking into account each other's constraints and specificity."

These efforts and building the relations have established more branded presence in the retailer shops, when entering most stores you see clearly marked branded areas. This has not been sufficient for some manufacturers as they started establishing the shop in shops.

The shop in shops are areas within a retailer shop that are totally branded and often fully supplied and built by the manufacturer. These areas can be seen as mini showrooms, and will display the brand at its best within a retail environment.

With the upcoming of the Internet the manufacturer also started providing more branded digital media, these to be used with the products or on brand specific pages on the retail web.

The next step for many brand manufacturers was to establish single brand showrooms or so called experience centers (see Figure 17 for some examples), these are fully owned and operated by the manufacturer, only they are not selling any goods. The main purpose is to present the product and brand at its best, and often also function as an example for the retailer how products can be displayed. These showrooms often offer activities for the consumer like product testing or taking part in a course on how to use the products in the best way, all of this in a branded environment to strengthen the consumer brand experience.

Figure 17 - Brand store examples Nokia, Bose, Levis, Apple, Nespresso, Sony (Google Images, accessed 16th of October 2010)

Moving from a non-selling environment, to a selling was for a number of manufacturers a logic next step. Some of the A-brands operate so called flagship stores in the popular part of the major city shopping centers. These stores sell the products of that brand and more important they create the full experience around the brand.

The efforts are all made to generate the highest return on the brand asset, and making sure the consumer has the full experience.

From the different approaches we can also take learning on how to sell direct to consumers. Based on the professional survey (see Figure 18) all indicated that before those companies went direct to consumers online they had established one or more channels that were selling directly to consumers, these were not always offering the same range as their to be launched on-line stores.

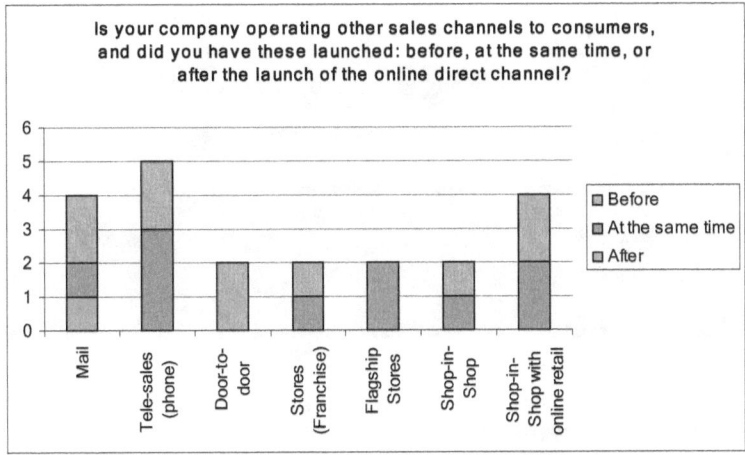

Figure 18 - Sales channels to consumers (Professional survey)

The data in Figure 18 shows that two manufacturers launched at the same time flagship stores as part of the go-live with direct sales to consumers. The key reason is that these manufacturers realized that they need physical presence of their goods, just having them on-line is not sufficient to create the branded image and make the consumer comfortable to buy directly on-line.

The online manufacturer shops are all very clearly branded and express the brand values, and create throughout the shopping process a branded experience. The consumer can clearly identify that he is shopping with the brand. When comparing a brand site with a standard retailer in that sells the same categories the biggest difference is the experience part of the site. The shopping journey starts on the home page, the home page has in all cases a rich experience that expresses the brand. The shopper can choose in the examples as shown in Figure 19 from the home page to enter the shop directly or enter the more experience driven pages that lead the consumer through the product features and help the consumer select the right product.

Figure 19 - Brand sites Nokia.com, Bose.com, Levis.com, apple.com, nespresso.com, sonystyle.com (Accessed 16th of October 2010)

The direct shop access from the main menu, provides a path to purchase that is supported by selection and filter tools, that support the consumer to find in a quick and easy way the product of his choice. These selection support features are driven by the key attributes of those product groups, for example for Levi's on jeans model, Nespresso coffee flavor, Sony tv's by screen size or technique, etc...

The two paths to purchase as mentioned, direct to the shop or the experience journey to find the product. It indicates that these manufacturers have created two paths to satisfy the consumer that knows what product it wants to purchase and those that are not yet sure what they need. This approach is aiming to drive optimal conversion in the on-line shop or generating traffic to the provided store addresses. The shops aim to follow a multi channel approach by providing guidance to different channels, and this indicates that none of these are following the channel absorption strategy.

Nespresso has an interesting approach as it provides links to shops where to buy the coffee machines, but for the coffee capsules they drive mainly to their own online sales, or their own boutiques that only sell the capsules.

4 Field research: Consumer expectations on Brand stores

Consumer insight has been gathered from a questionnaire that has been on-line for 10 days during September 2010, and the links were provided via email, on Linkedin and Twitter.

The survey questions were related to what the consumers expectations and experiences are with single brand stores, compared with multi brand stores. The stores can be physical stores or on-line.

In total 159 persons started the survey, of which 59% male and 41% female (based on the 148 respondents who answered that specific question), and for details on the age distribution see Figure 20. The males and the age group 35-44 is over presented, while no replies from younger than 18 and older that 65 years old. Due to this the outcome is not representative for the whole population, but most brands that sell durable goods have a focus on the age group above 25 due to their buying power, for this reason the results can be considered valid, but for interpretation reasons we need to keep in mind the demographics distribution.

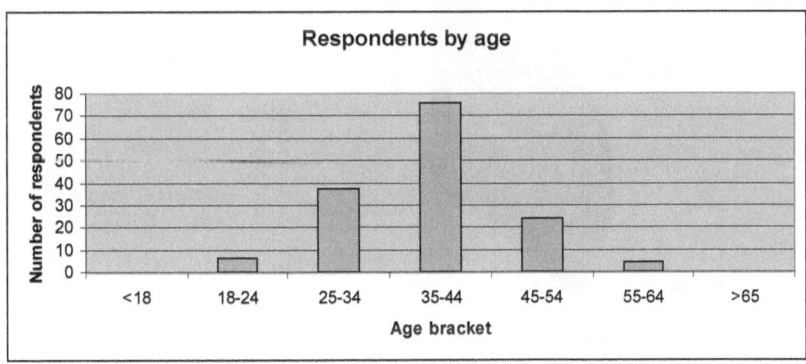

Figure 20 - Age brackets respondents (Consumer survey)

The following graphs in show the engagement of the respondents with shopping on-line (Figure 21) and their preference for brand stores (Figure 22):

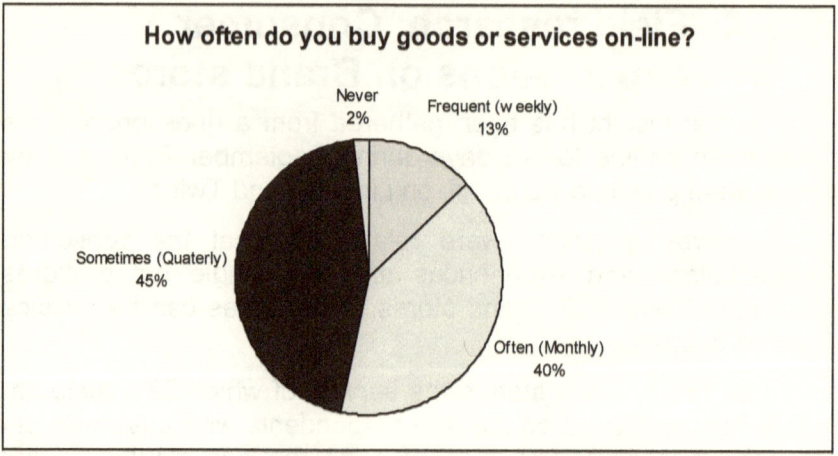

Figure 21 - Frequency of on-line purchases (Consumer survey)

The above graph show that the majority of the shoppers have almost all shopped on-line, most of the shoppers even do so often, only 1,9% percent never.

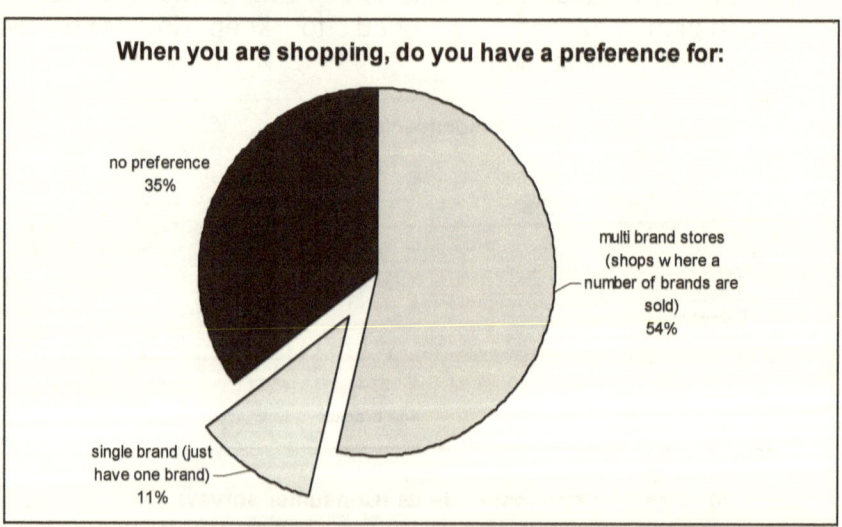

Figure 22 - Brand store preference (Consumer survey)

The survey indicates that the consumer has a preference for multi brand stores, only 11% indicates to have a preference for single brand stores. The preference for multi brand store or no preference for a single or multi brand store indicates that the shoppers shops for convenience at or need to have specific reasons to shop at a single brand store. The specific reason can be product related, the product dimension has not been part of this survey and therefore no conclusive answer can be given.

Figure 23 - Consumers that have bought from a brand store (Consumer survey)

The graph in Figure 23 indicates that the majority of the respondents have been shopping on-line or in physical stores that only carry one brand, even while this is not the preferred place to shop according to the data in Figure 22. The question arises what makes the single brand store interesting for the shopper, it is important for the manufacturer to know what elements the shop needs to differentiate on to attract shoppers. As mentioned earlier this can be product related, for some products the brand store is also the only available points of sales, for example Nespresso coffee.

According to the survey data these are to be found in the services and specific knowledge that multi brand stores do not provide or from a convenience (all assortment) point the shopper prefers to shop at a single brand store. Important element is also the trust and brand value are key differentiators as this the main asset that drives the consumer traffic to the stores.

From the survey outcome we can conclude that the main factors are for consumers to shop at single brand stores are the following three clusters, the underlying relations can be found in

Table 3. The variances explained by each factor range from 21.8% to 16.6%, for detailed explanation on the variances see Appendix 2. The clusters are based on the variances and the relation between the different factors that are important for the consumer to shop, as asked in question number four of the consumer survey.

The three main clusters for consumers to shop at a single brand store:

1. **Brand Equity and Ease of shopping** (consisting of Brand experience, trust and convenience)
2. **Value for money** (consisting of Knowledge and Price), positive related for knowledge and negative for price
3. **Store range** (existing of availability of brand related products and assortment)

Table 3 - Consumer reasons to buy from a brand store (Consumer survey)

Rotated Component Matrix

	Component		
	1	2	3
Brand experience	**.769**	.114	.262
Trust	**.706**	.246	.202
Convenience	**.607**	-.255	-.358
Knowledge	.218	**.745**	-.033
Price	.132	**-.721**	-.192
Service	.444	.524	-.208
Assortment	.150	.036	**.732**
Availability	.007	.002	**.690**

Extraction Method: Principal Component Analysis.
Rotation Method: Varimax with Kaiser Normalization.

The above mentioned factors are strongly linked to the brand equity and the manufacture strength supporting the brand. Most of these stores are true carriers of the brand values, for the brand owner they are often more than a point of sales but even more a way to strengthen the brand. Service, knowledge and assortment are elements to create that premium experience, in a branded environment.

The survey analyses resulted in one very interesting difference between male and female respondents. This difference is females rate the trust factor significantly higher of single brand stores compared to the male respondents, all the other reasons scored about the same. Trust is also the overall highest scoring item on question number four, making Trust in brand and products overall one of the main reasons to shop at a brand store, on-line or in the street.

In the questions five and six of the survey the service and price, see Figure 24 and Figure 25, were addressed and for service the outcome was consistent, as the consumer expected a higher than standard service compared to multi brand stores in a single brand store.

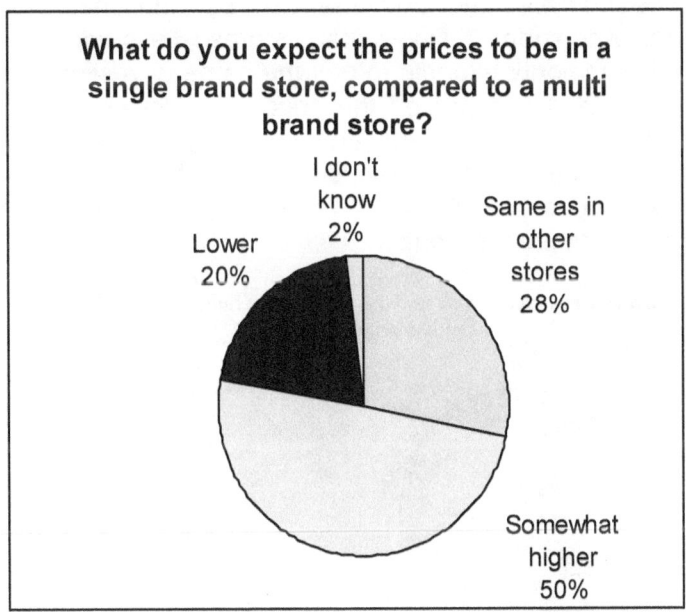

Figure 24 - Price expectations brand store (Consumer survey)

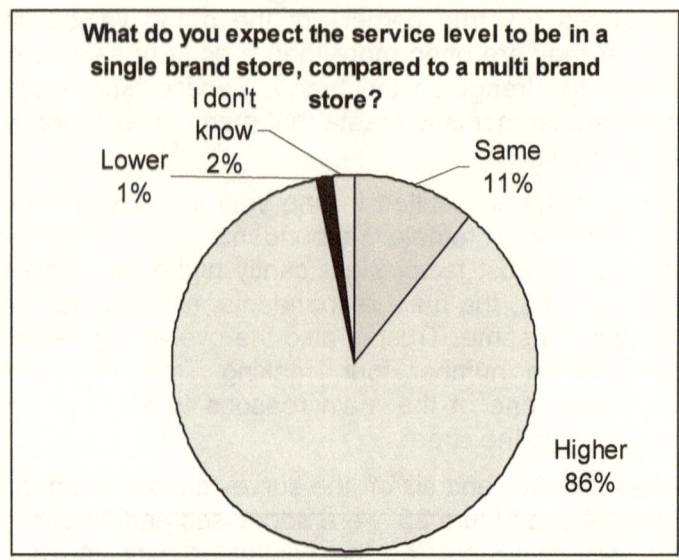

Figure 25 - Service level expectations in brand store (Consumer survey)

For price however the outcome can be explained that the consumer who shops in single brand stores is less price focused, but still the majority expects to pay the same or a slightly higher price, while 20,1% expected the price to be lower. The pricing would need further analyses and research to understand the elasticity for single brand stores, but most of the consumers don't seem to have perception that the brand stores are expensive or don't provide value for money.

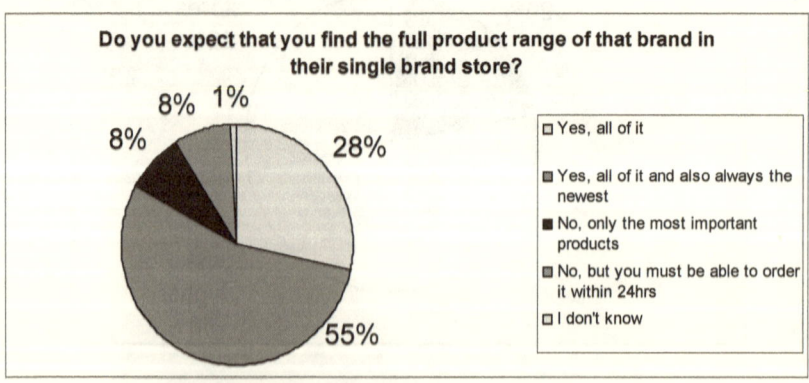

Figure 26 - Brand store range (Consumer survey)

The question on ranging gave some overall clear directions on what the respondents expect to find in the brand stores, as

83,1% expects to find the full brand range in the store, and 54,7% even expects to find also always the latest products.

The response on where to find the latest products the outcome was also rather clear, 40,9% expects these to be found in the on-line store of the brand, this is a clear indicator that the on-line stores are also the first place that people who are looking for the newest or the early adopters will search.

Only on if the products need to be branded (no other brands or white labels) in the store the outcome was undecided, as they all agree the products need to be related to the branded products sold. On the question number 8 can a brand store also sell other brands than the brand of the single store:

- 41,5% answered "No, as it is a single brand store I only expect their brand and that brand experience in store
- 42,1% answered "Yes, but only if the related to the branded products they sell"

Again behind this difference can be a link to the product category, this has not been investigated for this survey.

The ranging strategy to implement is most likely dependent on the category of products as for some products you can find unbranded but much related products that would fit very well for cross selling. Advised is to maintain the full brand experience it would be good to keep all the products in store branded and clearly in line with the overall brand strategy.

The question about what would be the main reason for a consumer to shop in a single brand store, was asked both in the consumer as in the professional survey

Interesting is to compare the outcome of what the consumer indicated and what the manufacturer expects to be the reasons that are important for the consumer. In Figure 27 the 4 main clusters of the reasons why it is important are compare with the professional and consumer survey. This is only a indication as the professional survey has a limited response and the electrical retail is overrepresented. Two main differences do stand out:

- Assortment: the professionals' rate assortment as more important, while consumer are not indicating this as most important this can be explained that consumers can view and purchase anyways the product in other stores. In general the products are widely available.

- Value for money: the consumers do value high knowledge and service for the right price as important, this even indicates that they are willing to pay more in the single brand stores, as long as there is good balance between the extra price and the services included.

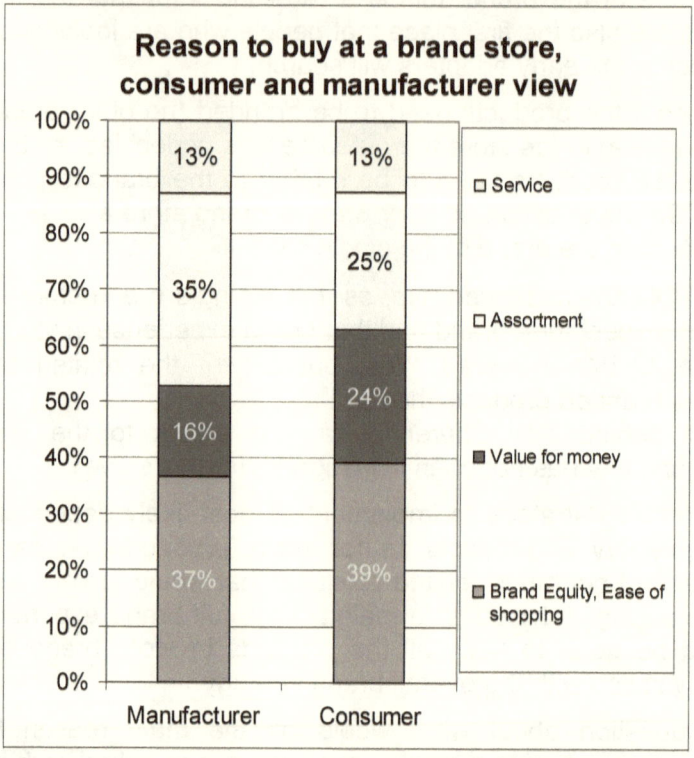

Figure 27 - Reasons to buy at brand store (Consumer and professional survey)

To conclude based on the survey data it indicates that the consumer has high expectations on service and assortment, full range and always the latest products in stock. The offering in the brand store, is seen as a bundle with a good value for money, consisting added value elements: convenience, knowledge and service. While the best brand experience is expected to be present in the single brand stores. This complimented by the trust factor of the brand, the trust is related to make sure the products are genuine and after-sales service elements.

Full details of the consumer and professional questions asked are in to be found in Appendix 1 and Appendix 3

5 Conclusions and Recommendations

The conclusions and recommendations are based on the material presented in this the thesis: the literature review, both surveys and current manufacturers' on-line practice. Most manufacturers are clearly active in the e-commerce space and have developed a strong web presence. The struggle and challenge is in some industries who will be the first mover to sell direct to consumers.

5.1 Conclusions

Based on the review of the market in chapter 2, the market environment is clearly in favor of e-commerce, as shown in Figure 4 the e-commerce forecast is close to 50% of the consumers will have shopped online by 2015. Internet has transformed the retail landscape and almost all retailers are now selling in a multi channel set-up.

The literature review resulted in a number of interesting and important findings, that are very important for the manufacture to understand and most of them indicate that the manufacturer has to be engaged with on-line sales. Schröder and Zaharia (2008) researched the multi channel consumer behavior, their research shows that the consumer behave differently based on the product they are looking to buy, and often they use the same channel they used for information for purchasing the product. Wolk and Skiera's (2009) research showed that adding an on-line channel has positive effects on the strategic and financial performance of the company. Channel cannibalization is often positive as volumes shift to a more profitable channel. The service levels will increase when a manufacturer adds a direct channel, as retail wants to be protected from being disintermediated, as explained by Yan et al. (2010).

Still many branded goods manufacturers have not taken the step to be actively engaged in on-line sales, and the Internet channel conflict is mentioned as the most common reason for not selling direct. Interesting is, that the channel conflict is mentioned in journals during the seventies, and Internet has created a new kind of channel conflict, based on information availability and that the channel power has shifted to the consumer. The consumer now decides in what channels to look for information and where to buy, the manufacturer needs to be present in the best possible way in all of those channels, including the direct channel.

Based on the consumer survey there are some clear reasons why the consumer would shop at single brand stores, but it also indicates it that a single brand store is not their preferred store. The main outcome of the questionnaire is that the consumer shops at a brand store because of the brand equity and ease of shopping. The brand experience and equity becomes the most important driver for consumers to shop at a single brand store. One other element was the convenience and service part, the consumer expects to find the full and latest range in the single brand store. The manufacturer must understand the consumer drive and the power of their brand, and what the consumer interest is for buying direct from the manufacturer. For the full details of the survey see chapter 4.

The manufacturer needs to make a number of decisions and organizational changes before they can sell direct to consumers. The strategic frameworks by Choi et al. (2009) and the model by Lee et al. (2001), as discussed in chapter 3.3, for manufacturer on-lines sales strategies, can both support the decision making process on what is the best strategy for on-line engagement. Both models suggest to the manufacturer, based on the input provided an on-line sales strategy to implement, from co-operation to quick transformation to only direct sales. The model as defined by Choi et all (2009) is for the author the preferred model, as it captures more the essence, channel and product, and suggest go-to market models for manufacturers, as Lee focuses only on channel conflict.

What is lacking in both models is how the return data flow can benefit the organization. This flow of direct consumer data can support the organization for improving products and processes, and therefore represents a value for the manufacturer.

The decision cannot be based on only considering the on-line channel set-up only, the manufacturer will have to take almost all processes and business stakeholders into account. To meet the consumer expectations it is important to understand their behavior, as they decide where to buy, for this it advised to gain consumer insight.

To conclude in line with the problem statement, what is the best strategy for a manufacturer to engage and even sell direct to consumers, with a positive effect on long term company results, as the Internet offers so many opportunities. The recommended direct on-lines sales strategic framework that is explained in the next paragraph will provide the guidance and decision models that the manufacture of durable goods can apply on their business.

5.2 Recommended direct on-line sales strategic framework

Companies that consider on-line presence on-line will need to define what strategy to implement. To be present on the Internet is nowadays a strategic must, or as Porter (2001) puts it: "Key question is not whether to deploy Internet technology, but how it should be deployed".

For deciding on the On-line sales strategy, the Strategic Management Process is recommended to structure the process. This process will aid to drive the right strategic choices and has as outcome an action plan that drives the implementation of the decided strategy. Each of the steps will be detailed resulting in a recommended working and decision framework for the on-line direct sales approach. By providing this framework the problem statement for this thesis will be answered: to provide the recommendation for manufacturers.

Strategic Management Process

Mission	1. **Mission**: What is the manufacturers' long term view of their Sales and Internet strategy, where does the company aspire to be in the long run and how does the brand strategy fit with the approach.
Objectives	2. **Objectives**: Measurable targets to what extent the organization is realizing the set out mission aspirations.

Business Analysis Internal & External	3.1 **External Analysis**: To identify the external critical threats and opportunities, in the competitive environment (market, retail, products, etc.) 3.2 **Internal Analysis**: Identify the manufacturer's strength and weaknesses (organizational, brand, products, etc.)
Strategic Choice	4. **Strategic Choice**: Decide on what strategy to implement and timeline, including understanding of the implications for the organization (Business plan)
Strategic Implementation	5. **Strategic Implementation**: develop processes and structures that are consistent with the strategic decision (Project plan)
Competitive Advantage	6. **Competitive Advantage**: measure and maintain to offer the consumers more value than competitors, by delivering a cost advantage or by differentiation

Mission

The key question that needs to be answered in this step is to have a clear mission statement for the on-line long term sales ambitions of the manufacture. This statement needs to cover the long term goals, and the "why?" on-line sales will contribute to these goals. In paragraph 3.2 a number of arguments are given that can support in defining the argumentation and mission statement.

Ideally the mission statement also defines what markets, brand and products that are within the scope as these are important constraints for defining the strategy. The brand position is also important as will it be used to build the brand or as traffic driver as discussed in chapter 3.4. In the mission the brand strategy needs to be clear and aligned as this will change when they plan to deal directly with consumers.

This statement will be the driver behind defining the objectives and deliverables for the on-line sales strategy. The final strategy decision will have a direct link to the mission; it will also give directions on how aggressive the manufacturer wants to be in order to accomplish their long term goals.

Objectives

Define how to measure the mission statement ambitions; these can be linked to the time to market, increase in market share, brand awareness, etc. The objectives will drive in more detail the on-line sales strategy. For example as explained in paragraph 3.4 what is the purpose of the on-line strategy, is it for building the brand or leveraging on the brand for direct sales, and what is the effect is on the brand value.

A part of setting the objectives is defining what the goal is clearly of developing the on-line sales strategy and what needs to be reached to have it become part of the sustainable competitive advantages for the company.

Analysis

Before the decision can be made on the strategy the internal and external environment should be analyzed to understand the how the strategy decision will benefit or impact the organization. The SWOT analysis is a one of the good tools to map this, but to capture the on-line specifics; there are some more elements to take into consideration.

External analysis

The External analysis must focus on the opportunities and threats of on-line sales. One key element is to compare and analyze the competitor or other business that can function as "best practice" examples. Most important external analyses for online sales are:

- On-line and e-commerce market statistics
- Web appropriateness of the product
- Pricing structure in the different channels

- Distribution structure, channel power and potential for channel conflicts
- Brand position and consumer expectations (see also the consumer survey data in chapter 4 on page number 65)
- Willingness from the consumer to buy direct from a brand sites

Internal analysis

The internal analysis must focus on the strengths and weaknesses of the organization in relation to on-line sales.

- Consumer relationship (CRM) and marketing management abilities
- Quality of web content and traffic to brand websites
- Brand power and marketing strategy
- IT systems available for On-line direct sales
- Organizational readiness to deal directly with consumers, for example pre- and after- sales interaction centers
- Supply chain abilities for consumer deliveries
- Reporting and legal requirements for consumer sales

Strategic Choice

Within the strategic choice two important decision need to be made first on what strategy to implement and secondly what time plan and phases, both based on a sound financial plan.

The strategic choice will be based on the in the earlier steps collected and analyzed data. As indicated the preferred model to decide web usage strategy is the model as developed by Choi et al. (2009), as discussed in chapter 4 for manufacturer on-lines sales strategies, see Figure 28 for the summarized graphical presentation of the model.

For defining the strategy the most important elements are:

1. Product appropriateness: can the product easily be sold on-line, as discussed in the literature review in chapter 2.2.
2. Channel conflict: would selling direct create a high or low channel conflict with the channel partners, channel conflicts are dealt with in chapter 2.6

3. Power: mainly driven by the brand strength has direct influence on both 1 and 2, as this creates trust for the product and also is needed for traffic driving to the stores, for details on Channel power see chapter 2.3.

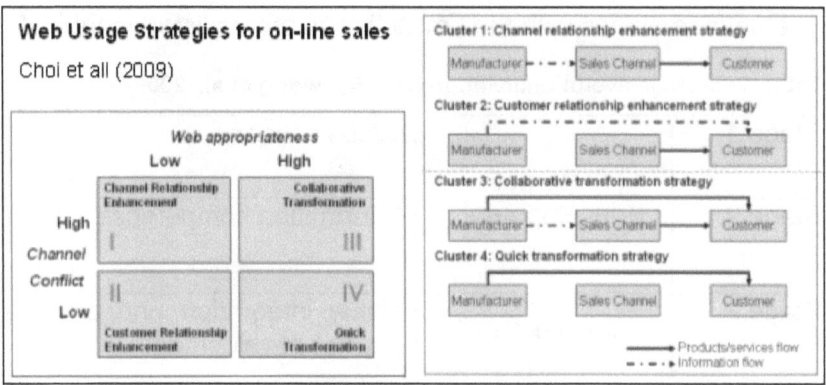

Figure 28 - Web usage strategies (Choi et al. 2009)

After defining the channel strategy that deals with direct sales, there needs to be a plan defined how to deal with channel conflicts. For this purpose the Decision-making framework to solve a channel conflict can be applied as defined by Bucklin (1997), see Figure 15. Important step is to calculate the net present value of the future cash flows with and without the new strategy, and investigate what channel is most affected, if any.

At this stage the manufacturer should also consider how to use or tap into the information the consumer can provide, and the value it represents to the organization.

Within the strategic decision, the implementation planning is important as the strategy can also be step wise implemented. Depending on the chosen strategy and organizational readiness the planning will be different, and based on this the efforts needed for implementation will differ. The first step of the planning is to understand where the organization is today in the different stages and where it wants to be, based on the strategy, and link to this a realistic planning.

The business case that will result out of the decisions made will be the guide to the next phase: the actual implementation of the strategy.

As an example the 5-stage evolutionary approach can be applied as defined by Ashworth et al. (2006) base on their analyses from brick to on-line sales organizations, for the full analyses and details see their report. In Appendix 5 a detailed example of the states and activities for each is included.

The defined stages with the key activities are as listed in table 4:

Table 4 - 5-Stage evolutionary approach (Ashworth et al., 2006)

Stage 1	Internet development	Web Presence
Stage 2		Information competence
Stage 3	On-line retail	Value integration and creative market development
Stage 4	Sustainable on-line retailing	Enhanced integration of skills, processes, technologies
Stage 5		Loyalty experience, learning and knowledge to maximize business value

Strategic implementation

After the decision is made on the strategy and planning, it will need to be implemented. The scoping and setting up the implementation team, is an important step for the manufacturer to develop the processes and functions that support and deliver successfully on the strategy.

The analyses of the value chain (see Figure 9) and define the fit-gap between the current and future processes will drive the planning, cost and execution. During the analyses phase there should already have been a high level fit-gap made and this can serve as base model.

To reach this result it is paramount for the manufacturer to understand the consumer expectations of the brand stores and what services, products and experience needs to present. The consumer survey, see chapter 4, indicates clearly that the consumer has a strong preference for brand stores based on:

1. **Brand Equity and Ease of shopping** (consisting of Brand experience, trust and convenience)

2. **Value for money** (consisting of Knowledge and Price), positive related for knowledge and negative for price
3. **Store range** (existing of availability of brand related products and assortment)

For the details see

Table 3, this table explains the above clusters linked to the consumer survey data.

During this phase the pre-, during- and after sales processes will need to be defined, and how these will marketed and accessible for the consumer. The branded experience needs to be available during the whole process for the consumer, as this is a clear outcome from the survey, as this creates trust and leads to conversion.

The business requirements for the business and IT platform will be closely linked by the brand experience and (self) service needs to be made available to the consumer.

Part of the implementation is also the measurement of success; based on the business intelligence the business performance needs to be measured. One of the great things of e-commerce is that the on-line consumer behavior can be measured during the shopping process, this will support conversion improvement changes.

Before the actual implementation the budgets and time plan needs to be reviewed.

Competitive advantage

After implementation the aim for the organization must be to maintain the competitive advantage and offer the consumers more value than the competition. The implemented strategy will need to be a driver for continuous improvement as retailing and consumer demands are changing faster than in the business to business environment.

To run an on-line sales business, the Internet site is not the most essential part of the competitive advantage, as this is just an fundamental element. The competitive advantages are currently mainly found in the consumer service, ability to customize during the process and quality of fulfillment. As an example of a company that is known and famous on the above elements is

Zappos.com (bought in 2009 by Amazon) they use as tag line: "powered by service", for example they ship orders, for free, within 2 hours after placement. Another example is CafePress they deliver within 24hrs consumer designed t-shirt, in the USA, according to an article by Hoffman (2008).

It will be very interesting to follow how mobile shopping and payments will develop (m-commerce) especially with the penetration of mobile Internet is now rapidly increasing in most markets, and of course the availability of smart phones and tablet pc's.

5.3 Manufacturer on-line strategy framework

The manufacturer has to collect, analyze and draw conclusions from the analyses that will lead to the strategic decision and implementation plan before they can define on how to develop their on-line sales engagement. To deal with this in a structured and fact driven approach the following framework is suggested; this presented in Figure 29 - Suggested Decision Framework.

This framework can be applied for all manufacturers that produce branded durable goods to decide on their on-line sales strategy, as a decision model on organizational level or for a specific market.

On-line direct Sales

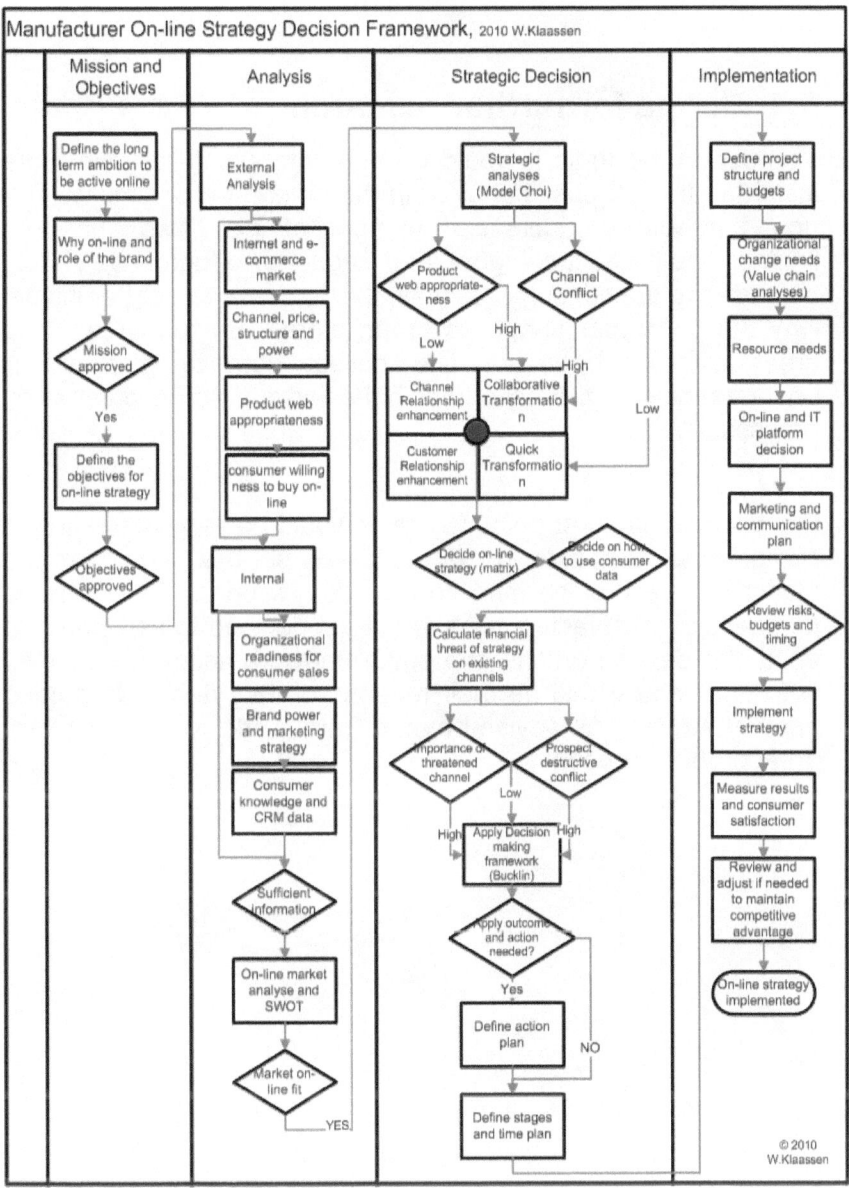

Figure 29 - Suggested Decision Framework

5.4 Scope for further research

To deepen the topic it would be very interesting to have more insight in the shopper behavior in the different e-commerce set-ups, this with an increased number of interviews and data mining. The product category, and frequency of purchase should be added to the consumer survey, this to gain even better insight why the consumer shops as brand stores. E-commerce offers great ways to measure and collect data to gain a full understanding of the consumer behavior during the purchasing process.

From a manufacturer point of view it would be very interesting to compare all the different direct sales set-ups, compare the platforms, back-office and front office support. Still a large numbers of manufacturers have not yet decided to sell direct, to apply the defined on-line strategy framework and see how they fit in and what would be their reasons of they decide to pursue another strategy as advised by the framework, would be a very great proof of concept.

6   Index of Appendixes

Appendix 1- Consumer survey

Brand Stores (MBA Thesis) - Consumer

1. Default Section

Hi, thank you for opening this questionnaire link about Brand shops, and what your experience is with them

The information provided will be used in my master thesis on Brand stores, as part of the EuroMBA study,if you leave your email address at the end, I will provide you with a summary of the outcome.

Just for clarification, when I mention a Single brand shop, these are shops where only 1 brand is sold, like Levi's, Apple, Nespresso, Sony, etc...

Your input is highly appreciated, so thanks in advance,
Wilko

1. How often do you buy goods or services on-line

○ Frequent (weekly)

○ Often (Monthly)

○ Sometimes (Quaterly)

○ Never

2. When you are shopping, do you have a preference for:

○ multi brand stores (shops where a number of brands are sold)

○ single brand (just have one brand)

○ no preference

3. Have you bought direct from a single brand shop (like Sony, Nespresso, Apple, Nike, Levi's, Bose, Philips, etc.)

○ Yes, from a street store

○ Yes, from their website

○ Yes, from their store and website

○ No, never

2. Brand Stores Experience

Brand Stores (MBA Thesis) - Consumer

4. What would be the main reason to shop at a single brand store, in the street or online (rate high 5 to low 1)

Rating

Availability of brand
related products

Service

Trust and quality of the
product

Knowledge and
information provided

Price

Assortment

Brand experience

Convenience (easy to buy
from)

Other (please specify)

5. What do you expect the prices to be in a single brand store, compared to a multi brand store?

O Same as in other stores

O Somewhat higher

O Lower

O I don't know

6. What do you expect the service level to be in a single brand store, compared to a multi brand store?

O Same

O Higher

O Lower

O I don't know

7. Do you expect that you find the full product range of that brand in their single brand store?

O Yes, all of it

O Yes, all of it and also always the newest

O No, only the most important products

O No, but you must be able to order it within 24hrs

O I don't know

Brand Stores (MBA Thesis) - Consumer

8. Can a single brand store also sell other brands than the store brand?

◯ yes, of course

◯ Yes, but only if related to the products they sell

◯ No, as it is single brand store I only expect their brand and that brand experience

◯ I don't know

9. Where would you expect to find the latest/newest products

◯ Any store that sells the brand

◯ On-line stores that sell the brand

◯ Single brand store on-line

◯ Single brand store in the street

10. When you buy the product in a brand store, do you expect a branded premium experience

◯ Yes, the shop needs to show the brand at its best

◯ Yes, but I don't expect to pay more for it

◯ No, just as a normal store

◯ I don't know

11. Any other comments or reflections on shopping from single brand stores

[   ]

3. Something more about you

12. Would you sign up for a brand store mailing to get always the latest products offered before they are in the store?

◯ Yes

◯ No

13. Can I know the following about you,

	Male/Female	Age (about)
I am ...	[ ]	[ ]

14. Please let me know something more about you, if you enter your e-mail address I provide you with a summary of the results.

Name:	[ ]
Country:	[ ]
Email Address:	[ ]

Appendix 2 - Variances explained (consumer survey)

Total Variance Explained

Component	Initial Eigenvalues			Rotation Sums of Squared Loadings		
	Total	% of Variance	Cumulative %	Total	% of Variance	Cumulative %
1	2.106	26.329	26.329	1.743	21.788	21.788
2	1.329	16.609	42.938	1.489	18.613	40.400
3	1.128	14.096	57.034	1.331	16.633	57.034
4	.890	11.131	68.165			
5	.796	9.952	78.117			
6	.728	9.095	87.212			
7	.573	7.162	94.374			
8	.450	5.626	100.000			

Extraction Method: Principal Component Analysis.

Appendix 3 - Professional survey

Direct sales to Consumer

Direct to Consumer Sales (MBA Thesis) Professionals

1. Default Section

Hi, thank you for opening this link for the questionnaire about direct sales to consumers, and what your experience is with selling to consumers. This research aims to give better insight in how brands are sold on-line, as I will report the findings back to you of this survey and also of the consumer survey version.

The information provided will be used in my master thesis on selling brands direct to consumers (online), as part of my EuroMBA study, if you leave your email address at the end, I will provide you with a summary of the outcome, and if you like more information you can contact me.

Professor C.Bechter, who is my tutor for this thesis, comments the following:
Internet provides the manufacturers of branded goods direct access to the consumer to promote and sell their products, however, the manufacturer faces the problem of benefiting from this possibility, strengthen the brand and cement consumer relations, Wilko's thesis in combination with the survey will provide more insight on the opportunities of direct sales of branded goods.

Your input is highly appreciated, so thanks in advance,
and I do plan to provide for who is interested access to the research data, and thesis, as to my knowledge their is not such research available.
Wilko
wilko.klaassen@euromba.org or wikla@yahoo.com

1. What is your relation to the consumer, I am a:

○ Manufacturer

○ Retailer

○ Consultant

○ Solution provider

○ Consumer, not having a business

○ Other (please specify)
[   ]

2. Do you have personally experience selling directly to the consumer via the internet (online)?

○ Yes, full range

○ Yes, only aftersales /service products (like: spares, consumables and accessories)

○ No, not with consumers only with B2B/Retail

○ Not yet, but soon we will start selling to consumers

○ Other (please specify)
[   ]

Direct to Consumer Sales (MBA Thesis) Professionals

3. What would be the main driver for a manufacturer to sell direct online to consumers (please rank 5- most important, 1 less important)

Rating

Marketing, more control and building the brand experience [ ]

Sales, additional sales channel [ ]

Retail power, establish a channel as alternative for retail oligopolies [ ]

Profit, overall improvement, profitable sales to consumers [ ]

Market entry, a way to establish distribution in a new market [ ]

Cross and Upselling, better capabilities [ ]

Consumer service, easy access to consumables and accessories [ ]

Consumer demand, the consumer expects to buy direct [ ]

Other (please specify)
[ ]

4. Is your company operating other sales channels to consumers, and did you have these launched: before, at the same time, or after the launch of the online direct channel?

	Before	At the same time	After
Mail	☐	☐	☐
Tele-sales (phone)	☐	☐	☐
Door-to-door	☐	☐	☐
Stores (Franchise)	☐	☐	☐
Flagship Stores	☐	☐	☐
Shop-in-Shop	☐	☐	☐
Shop-in-Shop with online retail	☐	☐	☐

Other (please specify)
[ ]

Direct to Consumer Sales (MBA Thesis) Professionals

2. Brand Stores Experience

5. How would you structure your brand store online (if you already have one, how is it structured?)

○ Separate online store

○ Fully integrated in your brand consumer site

○ Integrate in retail sites, with a specific shop-in-shop (maintained by the manufacturer/brand)

○ Integrate in retail sites, but maintained by the retailer

○ Other (please specify)

[_____]

6. If your company has more than one brand, would these be sold in a single or multi-brand store

○ Single

○ Multi

○ Differs by country

○ NA

7. Besides the main brand would you offer other products (not-branded or other brand) in the same shop

○ No, only branded products of the shop brand

○ Yes, only products that are directly related to the brand category (non-branded)

○ Yes, only products and brands that are directly related to the brand category and experience

○ Yes, any other product we can sell

○ NA

○ Other (please specify)

[_____]

Direct to Consumer Sales (MBA Thesis) Professionals

8. What would be the main reason for a consumer to shop at a single brand store, in the street or online (rate high 5 to low 1), while the brand is also available in multi brand stores/warehouses

	Rating
Assortment	[ ]
Availability of brand related products	[ ]
Brand experience	[ ]
Convenience (easy to buy from)	[ ]
Knowledge and information provided	[ ]
Price	[ ]
Service	[ ]
Trust and quality of the product	[ ]

Other (please specify)

[_____]

Direct to Consumer Sales (MBA Thesis) Professionals

3. Experience with retail and organizational setup

9. Have you experienced or do you expect any reaction by going direct to consumers from retailers (your b2b customers) or your organisation (Internal)?

	From Retail	From Internal
None	☐	☐
Negative, less orders	☐	☐
Negative, less floor space	☐	☐
Neutral, some negative some positive no measurable effect	☐	
Positive, increased orders and brand commitment	☐	☐
I don't know	☐	☐

Other (please specify)

[_____]

10. If Negative, Neutral or little channel conflict, can you briefly explain the key challenges and how you (plan to) deal with them:

[_____]

11. As a manufacturer selling direct has a number of challenges for the organization, what do you see as most challenging/important areas to take care of (1 low challenge - 5 high challenge)

	Rating
After sales service	[____]
Planning	[____]
Sales	[____]
Marketing	[____]
Resources	[____]
Customer relations	[____]
Sales	[____]
Logistics	[____]
Consumer service	[____]
Product range	[____]
Legal	[____]
Stock management	[____]

Other (please specify)

[_____]

12. For selling direct to consumers, do you operate the same platform globally?

◯ Yes   ◯ No   ◯ NA   ◯ Not Decided

Direct to Consumer Sales (MBA Thesis) Professionals

13. Any other comments you would like to add about direct to consumer online brands sales?

Direct to Consumer Sales (MBA Thesis) Professionals

4. Something more about you and your organisation

14. What industry are you working in?

[   ]

Other (please specify)

[   ]

15. what is your position or for what department are you working?

[   ]

16. The information you provide will be used for my research, can I mention your company

○ No

○ Yes (please specify)

[   ]

17. If you enter your e-mail address I will update you with the results of this questionnaire

Name: [   ]

Company: [   ]

Country: [   ]

Email Address: [   ]

Appendix 4 - Cluster analysis result (Choi et al., 2009)

Results of cluster analysis by K-means techniques.

Internet usage variables	Cluster 1	Cluster 2	Cluster 3	Cluster 4	Mean	p-Value
Web appropriateness	2.95 Low	2.71 Low	3.80 High	3.60 High	3.10	0.00
Channel conflict	3.60 High	2.95 Low	3.40 High	2.55 Low	3.25	0.00
Number of cases	24	21	11	7		

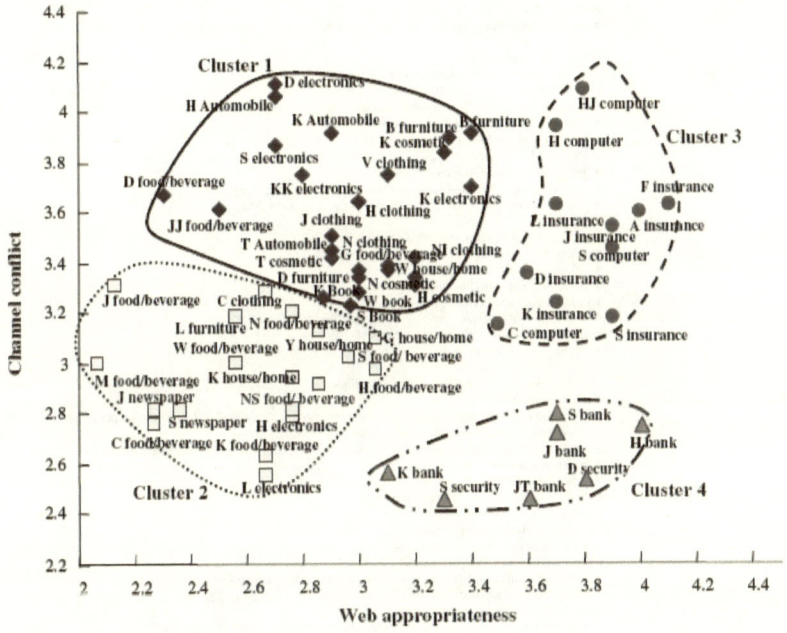

Appendix 5 - 5 stages evolutionary development (Ashworth et al., 2006)

Phase & timescales	Evolutionary development (Clicks-and-Mortar/Pure-Play)
Stage-1 • LUK: 1995–96 • LBW: 1998–99 • 2–6 months	Web presence • Minimal value added, minimal functionality • Costs minimized as company 'tests the water' • Investment made to 'continue' competing/broaden access to divergent markets • Limited understanding of technology, low competence levels • Ad-hoc monitoring/measurement • Pursuit of profit from the outset • Organizations bridge 'knowledge', followed by 'information competence' gaps prior to stage-2
Stage-2 • LUK: 1996–98 • LBW: 1999–2000 • 1–2 years	Information competence • Company experiences value of 'online' operation • Still 'experimental', back-office systems basic & separate • As online sales develop, requires more management attention & focus • Costs recouped, confidence in new-route to market grows • Operating with ad hoc strategy & limited direction, despite revenues • Desire to bring technology & control over IT in-house (minimizes costs, expands ELK & grows staff commitment) • Sales arena expanded (domestic, international) • Start utilizing offline knowledge in a more focused way: e.g. 'fitting' online [LUK] • Bridge 'organizational capabilities' gap (*Process, Product & Marketing*)
Stage-3 • LUK: 2000–02 • LBW: 2000–02 • 2–3 years	Value integration & creative market development • Improved functionality & technology development • Customization of product/service capabilities • Brand building & monitoring • Incremental added value to customers • Initiation, trial and monitoring of strategic/reciprocal links [LBW] • Joint marketing: e.g. community-sites [LBW]; fashion shows [LUK] • Bridge 'value integration' gap
Stage-4 • LUK: 2002–03 • LBW: 2002–03 • 1–2 years	Enhanced integration (of skills, processes, technologies) • Costs minimized • Integration of strategy and back-office support systems with offline [LUK]/across multiple-cyber stores [LBW] • Continued on/offline/intra-site joint promotional/branding activities • Introduce tailored service opportunities: customized product selection/manufacture [LBW]/mini-catalogues [LUK] • International online sales support domestic seasonalities • Links between multiple-sites and affiliates boost traffic/sales [LBW] • Enterprises bridge strategic transformation gap
Stage-5 • LUK: 2003 ff. • LBW: 2003 ff.	Leverage experience, learning & knowledge (ELK) to maximize business value • Consolidation & final leveraging solidifies 'Business Value' process • Maximize loyalty-effect, with quality & targeted focus • Consolidate internal structures & web-design, re-branding as required • Continual training keeps pace with market/technology developments • Maximum utilization of synergies & ELK • Value/revenue streams/opportunities reassessed securing long-term business value

Aspects of each development stage applies to all case websites unless otherwise stated.

7 References

7.1 Books, Articles and Research papers

Anderson, C., 2006, *The Long Tail: Why the Future of Business Is Selling Less of More.*, Hyperion

Ashworth, C., Schmidt R., Pioch E. and Hallsworth A., 2006, An approach to sustainable 'fashion' e-retail: A five-stage evolutionary strategy for 'Clicks-and-Mortar' and 'Pure-Play', *Enterprises,Journal of Retailing and Consumer Services 13*, pp.289–299

Brook, P. and Poich, E., 1996,*The strange case of home shopping in and the single European market, Journal of Retailing and Consumer Services Vol.3 No.3*, pp.175-182

Bucklin, C. et all, 1997, Channel conflict: when is it dangerous?, *McKinsey Quarterly 3*, pp. 36-43

Burt, S. and Sparks, L., 2003, E-commerce and the retail process: a review, *Journal of Retailing and Consumer Services (Elsevier)*, pp.275–286

Chang, K-H. and Gotcher, D., 2010, Conflict-coordination learning in marketing channel relationships: The distributor view, *Industrial Marketing Management 39*, pp.287–297

Choi B., Hong, J-W. Lee, C. and Lee, H., 2009, Deriving web usage strategies for online sales: A decision framework and empirical exploration, *Expert Systems with Applications 37*, pp.3695–3705

Coelho, F. and Easingwood, C., 2008, A model of the antecedents of multiple channel usage, *Journal of Retailing and Consumer Services 15*, pp.32–41

Dupuis, M. and Tissier-Desbordes, E., 1996, Trade marketing and retailing: a European approach, *Journal of Retailing and Consumer Services Vol 3*, No 1, pp.43-51

Engel, J.F. et al., 1995, *Consumer Behavior*, Hinsdale

Hoffman, W., 2008, From bricks to clicks, Dec. 22, *The journal of commerce*

Iyer, G., 1998, Coordinating Channels Under Price and Nonprice Competition, *Marketing Science, Vol. 17*, No.4

Jelassi, T. and Leenen, S. 2003, An E-Commerce Sales Model for Manufacturing Companies, *European Management Journal Vol. 21, No. 1*, pp.38–47

Juhl H., Esbjerg K., Grunert K. Bech-Larsen T. and Brunsø K., 2006, The fight between store brands and national brands. What is the score?, *Journal of Retailing and Consumer Services 13*, pp.331–338

Jupiter Research, 2009, Selling Direct To Consumers Online: Channel Conflict Or Opportunity?, *Research report by Jupiter Research for Digital river* (January, 2009)

Lee, Y., Lee, Z. and Larsen, K.RT., 2001, Coping with Internet Channel Conflict, *Communication of the ACM*, Vol. 46, No.7 pp.137 – 142

Markides, C., D. and Charitou, C., (2004). Competing with dual business models: A contingency approach. *Academy of Management Executive, vol.18, No3*, pp 22-36

Marmorstein, H., Rossomme J. and Sarel, D., (2003). Unleashing the power of yield management in the Internet era., *California Management Review, vol. 45, No 3*, pp 1-22

Park, J., Chung, H. and Sang Yoo, W., 2009, Is the Internet a primary source for consumer information search?: Group comparison for channel choices, *Journal of Retailing and Consumer Services 16*, pp.92–99

Parment, A., 2008, Distribution strategies for volume and premium brands in highly competitive consumer markets, *Journal of Retailing and Consumer Services 15*, pp.250–265

Porter, M., 1985, *Competitive advantage*, Free Press, New York

Rahim, M.A., 2000, Managing *Conflict in organizations*, Quorum Books Westport

Schröder, H. and Zaharia, S., 2008, Linking multi-channel customer behavior with shopping motives: An empirical investigation of a German retailer, *Journal of Retailing and Consumer Services 15*, pp.452–468

Umit Kucuk, S. and Krishnamurthy, S., 2007, An analysis of consumer power on the *Internet, Technovation 27*, pp.47–56

Vinhas, A. and Anderson, E., Nov. 2005, How Potential Conflict Drives Channel Structure: Concurrent (Direct and Indirect) Channels, *Journal of Marketing Research, Vol, XLII*, 507-515

Wolk, A. and Skiera, B., 2009, Antecedents and consequences of Internet channel performance, *Journal of Retailing and Consumer Services 16*, pp.163–173

Yan, R. and Pei, 2009, Retail services and firm profit in a dual-channel market, Journal *of Retailing and Consumer Services 16*, pp.306–314

Yan, R., Wang, J. and Zhou, B., 2010, Channel integration and profit sharing in the dynamics of multi-channel firms, *Journal of Retailing and Consumer Services*

7.2 Web pages

1. http://www.buzzle.com/articles/online-shopping-trends.html accessed on 4th of September 2010

2. http://www.ebayinc.com/who accessed on the 4th of September 2010

3. http://phx.corporate-ir.net/phoenix.zhtml?c=176060&p=irol-mediaKit Accessed on the 4th of September 2010

4. http://www.dell.com/content/topics/global.aspx/about_dell/company/history/history?c=us&l=en Accessed on the 4th of September 2010

5. http://news.sel.sony.com/en/corporate_information/company_of_firsts

6. http://www.businessweek.com/technology/content/mar2010/tc2010034_952664.htm

7. http://www.Internetretailer.com/2010/09/24/online-shoppers-are-spending-more-time-manufacturer-web-sites accessed on the 25th of September 2010

8. http://www.davechaffey.com/E-commerce-Internet-marketing-case-studies/Boo.com-case-study accessed on the 9th of October 2010

9. http://www.retailonlineintegration.com/article/five-characteristics-successful-multichannel-merchandiser-90252/1 accessed on the 16th of October 2010

10. http://www.businessweek.com/ap/financialnews/D9IRFPDO2.htm accessed on the 16th of October 2010

11. http://www.Internetretailing.net/2010/09/hm-online-arrives-in-the-uk/ accessed on the 16th of October 2010

12. http://www.ft.com/cms/s/0/05b87696-b5e4-11df-a048-00144feabdc0.html accessed on the 16th of October 2010

13. http://uk.reuters.com/article/idUKTRE61000G20100201 accessed on the 16th of October 2010

14. http://www.direct2consumeronline.com/aboutD2C_benefits_concerns.php accessed on the 16th of October 2010

8 About the Author and Thesis

The author Wilko Klaassen, born in 1976, finished in 2011 his Executive MBA, before he followed education in the Netherlands and Denmark, both in Business and Economics. He has been working since 1999 and been based in several European countries, and has global work experience.

Wilko has been active since 1999 with Internet related activities, from developing websites, e-business products, heading the e-commerce channel and launching web shops for large cooperations (SCA Packaging and Electrolux). His roles are in general focused on business development, process optimization and interaction with the customers, with as goal to unlock profit opportunities. Currently he is employed at Electrolux at their global HQ as Director of commercial development of on-line sales to consumers.

As part of the Euro*MBA graduation requirements exist the requirement to write a final thesis, that covers the different topics studied and how to apply these to a business challenge. The topic of his MBA thesis is mainly a Business Consulting Project that looks into business challenges and opportunities for direct sales, supported by actual cases, literature studies and field surveys.

Contact the author: m2c@wklaassen.nl

About the EURO*MBA

The Euro*MBA is a truly European programme for internationally oriented managers and professionals, designed and realized by a consortium of six European universities/business schools of outstanding calibre.

The Euro*MBA fits the needs of the current executive to combine theoretical and practical training and work, allowing them to study from home, yet to work with executives from around the world. Since its inception in 1996, flexibility, high quality theoretical and practical training, innovative work processes and international network have been the keywords of the Euro*MBA programme

This international Euro*MBA leads to the MBA degree of the full consortium members:

Euro*MBA Consortium:

- AUDENCIA Nantes, Ecole de Management; France

- Institut d 'Administration des Entreprises (IAE), l'Université Paul Cézanne; France

- Escuela de Alta Dirección y Administración (EADA); Spain

- HHL Leipzig School of Management; Germany

- Leon Kozminsky Academy of Entrepreneurship and Management (LKAEM); Poland

- Universiteit Maastricht Business School, Faculty of Economics and Business, Universiteit Maastricht; Netherlands

The Euro*MBA programme is:

- AMBA accredited (programme accreditation)

- AACSB accredited via Maastricht University, HHL - Leipzig Graduate School of Management and AUDENCIA Nantes School of Management (school accreditation)

- EQUIS accredited via IAE Aix Graduate School of Management, AUDENCIA Nantes School of Management, EADA - Escuela de Alta Direccion y Administracion Barcelona and Kozminsky University Warsaw (school accreditation).